Modern India: A Very Short Introduction

VERY SHORT INTRODUCTIONS are for anyone wanting a stimulating and accessible way into a new subject. They are written by experts, and have been translated into more than 45 different languages.

The series began in 1995, and now covers a wide variety of topics in every discipline. The VSI library now contains over 500 volumes—a Very Short Introduction to everything from Psychology and Philosophy of Science to American History and Relativity—and continues to grow in every subject area.

Very Short Introductions available now:

ACCOUNTING Christopher Nobes
ADOLESCENCE Peter K. Smith
ADVERTISING Winston Fletcher
AFRICAN AMERICAN RELIGION
    Eddie S. Glaude Jr
AFRICAN HISTORY John Parker and
    Richard Rathbone
AFRICAN RELIGIONS Jacob K. Olupona
AGEING Nancy A. Pachana
AGNOSTICISM Robin Le Poidevin
AGRICULTURE Paul Brassley and
    Richard Soffe
ALEXANDER THE GREAT
    Hugh Bowden
ALGEBRA Peter M. Higgins
AMERICAN HISTORY Paul S. Boyer
AMERICAN IMMIGRATION
    David A. Gerber
AMERICAN LEGAL HISTORY
    G. Edward White
AMERICAN POLITICAL HISTORY
    Donald Critchlow
AMERICAN POLITICAL PARTIES
    AND ELECTIONS L. Sandy Maisel
AMERICAN POLITICS
    Richard M. Valelly
THE AMERICAN PRESIDENCY
    Charles O. Jones
THE AMERICAN REVOLUTION
    Robert J. Allison
AMERICAN SLAVERY
    Heather Andrea Williams
THE AMERICAN WEST Stephen Aron
AMERICAN WOMEN'S HISTORY
    Susan Ware

ANAESTHESIA Aidan O'Donnell
ANARCHISM Colin Ward
ANCIENT ASSYRIA Karen Radner
ANCIENT EGYPT Ian Shaw
ANCIENT EGYPTIAN ART AND
    ARCHITECTURE Christina Riggs
ANCIENT GREECE Paul Cartledge
THE ANCIENT NEAR EAST
    Amanda H. Podany
ANCIENT PHILOSOPHY Julia Annas
ANCIENT WARFARE Harry Sidebottom
ANGELS David Albert Jones
ANGLICANISM Mark Chapman
THE ANGLO-SAXON AGE John Blair
ANIMAL BEHAVIOUR
    Tristram D. Wyatt
THE ANIMAL KINGDOM
    Peter Holland
ANIMAL RIGHTS David DeGrazia
THE ANTARCTIC Klaus Dodds
ANTISEMITISM Steven Beller
ANXIETY Daniel Freeman and
    Jason Freeman
THE APOCRYPHAL GOSPELS
    Paul Foster
ARCHAEOLOGY Paul Bahn
ARCHITECTURE Andrew Ballantyne
ARISTOCRACY William Doyle
ARISTOTLE Jonathan Barnes
ART HISTORY Dana Arnold
ART THEORY Cynthia Freeland
ASIAN AMERICAN HISTORY
    Madeline Y. Hsu
ASTROBIOLOGY David C. Catling
ASTROPHYSICS James Binney

Available soon:

For more information visit our website

www.oup.com/vsi/

Craig Jeffrey

MODERN INDIA

A Very Short Introduction

OXFORD
UNIVERSITY PRESS

OXFORD
UNIVERSITY PRESS

Great Clarendon Street, Oxford, OX2 6DP,
United Kingdom

Oxford University Press is a department of the University of Oxford.
It furthers the University's objective of excellence in research, scholarship,
and education by publishing worldwide. Oxford is a registered trade mark of
Oxford University Press in the UK and in certain other countries

© Craig Jeffrey 2017

The moral rights of the author have been asserted

First edition published in 2017

Published in the United States of America by Oxford University Press
198 Madison Avenue, New York, NY 10016, United States of America

British Library Cataloguing in Publication Data
Data available

Library of Congress Control Number: 2017942730

ISBN 978–0–19–876934–7

Printed and bound by
CPI Group (UK) Ltd, Croydon, CR0 4YY

To Jane, Florence, and Finn

Contents

Acknowledgements

I am extremely grateful to Trent Brown for research assistance provided in association with the production of this book. I thank Jenny Nugee, Andrea Keegan, Saraswathi Ethiraju and Erica Martin at Oxford University Press for their help. I am also most grateful to Robin Jeffrey, Glyn Davis, Amanda Gilbertson, Assa Doron, Souresh Roy, Brigid Freeman, Jonathan Balls, Amy Piedalue, Jane Dyson, and other colleagues at the University of Melbourne and Australia India Institute for reading drafts of the book. I also thank Dorothy McCarthy for her editorial work. None bears any responsibility for errors and omissions that remain.

List of illustrations

Chapter 1
Hope

A few years ago there was a traffic hold up in the town of Karnaprayag in Uttarakhand, north India. Trucks, cars, and bicycles snaked along the mountain road that runs through the settlement. Many drivers gave up waiting inside their vehicles. They ambled along the queue sipping chai. Others searched for the source of the traffic jam. At the crossing of the Ganges River in the centre of the town, a group of schoolchildren had stopped the traffic. Sitting in a circle on the bridge with their arms locked together they chanted their main demand and sang popular local Garhwali songs. They wanted a better maths teacher at their school. The current one was not turning up regularly to classes. The children felt it was their right to be taught by a competent teacher—'It Is Our Constitutional Right', read one of their placards. The police hovered at the edge of the demonstration, threateningly tap-tapping their *lathis* (wooden sticks) against the side of the bridge. After a few hours, the District Magistrate (DM) arrived at the scene. A heated conversation, more songs, and a speech by a sympathetic schoolteacher followed the DM's arrival. Three weeks later, a new maths teacher arrived at the school.

One would not—at first blush—expect India to be short of effective maths teachers. India is the fastest growing major economy in the world with a large and rapidly growing middle class. In some respects, India is the last among the so-called

BRICS (Brazil, Russia, India, China, and South Africa) to have remained strong. Brazil's economy is in a state of profound crisis. Russia and South Africa's Gross Domestic Product (GDP) is growing very slowly and even China's rate of growth is in decline.

It is not just growth. India looks generally healthy from an economic standpoint. India's balance of payments is under control and it has established an identity as a major power in terms of Information Technology (IT). It remains robust in other sectors—such as real estate, construction, pharmaceuticals, and gemstones—and is showing some growth in energy and manufacturing. In 2015, Moodys changed India's economic outlook from 'stable' to 'positive'.

To list more reasons for optimism: Indian economic growth has reduced poverty; the literacy rate has risen sharply; and cultural and arts industries are flourishing—not only within the country, but also globally. India has a large and successful diaspora population.

With economic growth comes greater political influence. India has developed a reputation as a global player in terms of foreign policy. It is increasingly a type of 'superpower' with a responsibility to lead in the political realm throughout the Asia-Pacific, counterbalancing the regional influence of China and the United States. India has rejected foreign aid and become, itself, a global donor. Since the mid-1990s, India has dramatically increased its aid contributions to poor countries in South Asia and some parts of Africa.

Yet India's impressive growth story is fraught with contradictions. It has a GDP per capita below that of Sudan. Economic reforms in India, which began in the 1980s and gathered pace in the 1990s, widened social inequalities across the subcontinent. India remains a country containing a staggering number of people who are identified—or self-identify—as 'poor'.

Commentators tend to think of Africa as the place of the most extreme poverty in the world. Yet it is India that is home to 37 per cent of the world's adult illiterates. Child undernourishment typically affects about 20 per cent of children in sub-Saharan Africa, but it affects roughly 30 per cent of children in India. The poorest eight Indian states are actually worse off than the poorest sub-Saharan African nations, a point that has led some commentators to identify an 'India within India' or 'fourth world' of 'sick' Indian states. Such observations become still more distressing when one considers gender and other inequalities, such as caste. Those who occupy low positions in multiple social hierarchies, such as 'untouchable' women in rural north India, face major challenges acquiring even basic amenities.

In the political sphere, too, the cliché about India being a country of contradictions is largely true. India is often celebrated as the world's largest democracy. It has regular elections and the rule of law. There are routine changes of government, reflecting people's altering political views and preferences. Very large numbers of people vote—66 per cent in the 2014 elections. India also has some strong institutions: the Supreme Court, the Electoral Commission, the Comptroller and Auditor General, Reserve Bank of India, and the civil service, for example.

The subcontinent has also become more democratic in the seventy years since Independence. Parties representing India's lowest castes have been successful in India's most populous state, Uttar Pradesh. In the 2010s, a party claiming to articulate the views of people dissatisfied with the political establishment—the Aam Aadmi (Ordinary Person's) Party—achieved success.

India is possibly the only country in the world where the print media is expanding. Civil society is strong, too. There are numerous non-governmental organizations (NGOs) scattered across India that are pursuing democratic objectives. The 21st century has witnessed the rise of different movements proclaiming people's rights—to food, education, and work, for example—and their right to live in a country that is not corrupt.

This democratic success is astonishing—some have termed it a 'miracle'—given that in 1947 India was a poor, illiterate country that had suffered from the ravages of colonial rule. Political theory dictates that most of the requirements for successful democratic functioning—a strong growing economy, vibrant civil society, and public education—were lacking in India when it became an independent country in 1947. Even one of the main architects of the Indian Constitution, the low-caste political leader Dr Bhimrao Ambedkar, predicted that India's democracy might well fail. Political theorists and many British commentators wrote about how the former colony would crumble under the weight of its contradictions. India's democratic success is surprising, too, when read against the experiences of its neighbour, Pakistan, which has experienced several periods of military rule.

But there is a dark side to India's political trajectory. The legal system has a backlog of gargantuan proportions. Corruption and malpractice are rife within Indian government bureaucracies, including the police. There are serious concerns about freedom of expression in India, evident in 2016 in a heavy-handed government crackdown on students protesting at India's historically left-wing Jawaharlal Nehru University (JNU) in Delhi and in Hyderabad University in south India. India may be a successful formal democracy but people from marginalized backgrounds are often unable to participate in political discussions and representative government.

India is also a place of opposites in the social sphere. The subcontinent is poised to benefit from a demographic dividend: a large youth population that could drive further economic growth. This youth population is better educated than were previous generations and better linked to communication technologies and flows of ideas, information, and people from outside the subcontinent. Yet, many young people in India feel frustrated by poor infrastructure, corruption, a lack of state assistance, and the failure of the Indian economy to create jobs. The education system in India remains poor. Schools suffer from a lack of curricular reform, teacher absenteeism, and widespread underfunding. Public universities are in a parlous state. Moreover, most Indian citizens cannot obtain effective healthcare.

Ordinary lives

The importance of poverty, inequality, and exclusion in contemporary India becomes clearer when one considers people's ordinary lives. Take Prempal Singh, a 33-year-old man living in the village of Bemni. Bemni is located in the Nandakini Valley in the mountainous north Indian state of Uttarakhand. The village is located at 10,000 feet and lies close to the border of Tibet. It is remote, but in many respects exemplifies processes occurring in other parts of village India.

Bemni changed dramatically in the first decade of the 21st century. A road was constructed to the village for the first time. It acquired an irregular supply of electricity. The government schools in Bemni were extended and a mobile phone tower was constructed. In the meantime, agriculture declined, reflecting the effects of climate change, the commendation of land for construction, and a general lack of interest in farming among young people.

Prempal Singh lives with his wife and two children in Bemni. Prempal was educated locally and then studied for a BA and MA in English Literature at local universities. He could not afford to travel to the universities to study and enrolled instead in correspondence courses. Prempal cannot acquire any of the books, such as George Eliot's *Silas Marner* and Charles Dickens's *Great Expectations*, which form the backbone of his MA degree. These books are not stocked locally and the universities do not send them to the students working by correspondence. Instead he buys books from the local bazaar that contain sample answers in English to questions that will appear on the exam. Unable to speak English well, Prempal memorizes the answers he finds in textbooks.

Prempal also farms his modest patch of land. He works on a voluntary basis as a teacher in the local credit association. He also participates in a government employment programme: the Mahatma Gandhi National Rural Employment Guarantee Scheme, which provides him with about forty days of paid work every year (it is supposed to be 100 days but it is not implemented effectively). In addition, Prempal walks up to the high pastures at 16,000 feet altitude to collect caterpillar fungus, which is sold to local traders and used as an aphrodisiac in China.

Through these various forms of entrepreneurialism Prempal Singh makes ends meet. 'I adjust,' he said. But Prempal retains hope that a secure government job may materialize before too long. 'I continue to hope. The world runs on hope,' he pointed out. His chances of success seem slim. In 2012 there were over 86,000 applications for 79 new positions in the Uttarakhand state government.

In the meantime, Prempal Singh has become a community leader, buoyed by his belief in hope. He campaigned for infrastructural improvements to the village, focusing especially on the three resources that he said are necessary for community development: education, infrastructure, and health facilities. He saw himself as a type of motivator in the village, assisting others with health emergencies, social disputes, and educational problems. He referred to himself as a 'hope machine'.

Prempal feels that his life is one of contradictions. There is development, he says, and he is optimistic that technological change in the future will improve people's lives. But social and economic change has also come with costs: unemployment, environmental degradation, and new conflicts between parents and children over education, relationships, and work. For Prempal Singh, these contradictions are lived realities. He can get mobile reception, but frequently has difficulties charging his phone. He has a right to demand access to good healthcare, but the doctor who is supposed to come to the village to work rarely arrives. He was interested in science as a child, but he said that there were no science teachers in any of the schools that serve the villages of the Nandakini Valley, including Bemni. If you are a science teacher, you are in high demand and you can manoeuvre to avoid being posted in a remote location.

Hemlata Singh is also in her early thirties but she lives in a more populous and better-connected part of India: the city of Meerut in Uttar Pradesh. Meerut is a city of great historical interest, with a famous Muslim core and a large army cantonment built by the British. The so-called 'Indian Mutiny' began in Meerut.

Hemlata lives in a middle-class suburb in the city. She was enrolled as a media student at a local university while also trying to address gender issues in the city. Hemlata developed her media training through writing articles on the need to improve security for young women on university campuses. She also campaigned to create separate seating areas for women on buses in the city.

On one occasion, an educational entrepreneur made the mistake of hiring Hemlata as an adviser. The man was seeking to establish a private school in a nearby district. He saw that Hemlata was bright and thought she could act as a shield in his attempts to establish an institution which prioritized making money over the educational needs of students. But Hemlata refused to undertake this role once it became clear what she would be doing. She told the entrepreneur that her intention was to end corruption not defend it.

Hemlata tried to change her local environment. 'I have hope,' she said. Hemlata believed that India was changing for the better. She said that there is a spirit of entrepreneurialism among people that was lacking ten years ago. Yet she was often downhearted. She said that police officers and senior government officials refuse to take her seriously and that as a woman in India she continues to face harassment.

Now consider Minu Singh who lives in the village of Manpur in rural Meerut district, in Uttar Pradesh. Minu is in her early fifties and comes from a low-caste, poor background. The roof of her house collapsed during a storm and she has not managed to have it repaired. A state officer came to assess the damage and arrange government compensation, but Minu did not appreciate how she was meant to handle the visit of the official. She did not even know who he was or his official designation. He went away without being paid the necessary bribe and Minu's house remains without a roof.

The incident was just one among a litany of similar instances in which Minu had felt herself powerless. She was unable to stop a wealthy local farmer of higher caste background harassing her niece in a field. She was not able to say anything when higher-caste women ostentatiously hitched up their saris when passing her house. 'They were clearly disrespecting me, but what could I do?' She feels socially isolated; recounting a popular north Indian phrase, she said: 'Even the dogs don't approach the empty-handed.'

Minu stressed the continued importance of caste discrimination in India. 'They do not abuse us openly', she said, 'but they do such wicked things behind our backs. And they pay us nothing but green fodder for the work we do in the fields.' The rich local farmers often managed to press low castes into service, paying them only pouches of liquor or fodder for their animals in return for a day's work.

Minu thought that there had certainly been progress in Manpur village since the times of her childhood in the 1960s, with the establishment of new classes in the school, improved transport to the local town, and more money being disbursed through local government. But she said that the continuities from the past were equally evident: continued caste discrimination, economic exploitation, crime, and corruption. 'Poverty is all these things,' she said, 'And more.' She continued plaintively: 'Who will cry about our sadness? How can we explain how poverty wears us down?'

Minu's neighbour Afrozi, a Muslim woman in her forties, said that for Muslims in the village expectations of upward mobility were even lower. 'Hindus in general are in a much better situation,' she said. 'My house has been broken for three years and still there is no one to help. I have decided that it is just a question of living out this life, knowing that the afterlife will be glorious.' She continued, 'There is Hindu discrimination everywhere, and even the (Hindu) schoolteacher will not teach my children properly. First we had the slavery of the British, now we experience slavery based on religion and caste.'

Inequality and hope

These examples tell a depressing tale of modern India. India is successful economically, but this has not translated into greatly enhanced living conditions for many Indians, who live in villages and small towns and who count themselves among the poor and lower middle class. This would include Prempal, possibly Hemlata, and certainly Minu and Afrozi.

Corruption and inequality saturate the everyday social scene, not only exacerbating tensions between the haves and have-nots but also sparking conflict within families. One of the most heart-rending aspects of living and working in modern provincial India is seeing how social change has pitted parents against their children and vice versa, as for example when young people ask, 'Why did you educate me where there are no jobs?' And parents reply: 'I sacrificed everything for your education, why aren't you grateful?' Economic growth has been notoriously bad in terms of generating jobs in the economy. Indeed, the period between 2004 and 2010—an interval that saw several years of double-digit growth—witnessed no improvement in job creation in India.

What is also evident is how such lived contradictions manifest themselves as tensions in people's own minds. Prempal feels torn between pursuing his goal of getting a government job and concentrating solely on working for his family in the village. Hemlata continues to work hard to try to expose gender injustice in the city but as a woman she finds that she is often not taken seriously in government offices. Minu is charged with feelings of anger about caste inequality, but she cannot channel this anger into obtaining resources from the government or confronting higher castes. Small wonder that the English word 'tension' has become lingua franca in many parts of India, used as a verb ('don't tension me'), adjective ('that was a very tension conversation'), and noun ('stop giving me tension').

But there is also hope. Seventy years of Independence have somehow fostered in people's minds the idea that the state can and should assist them and that 'poverty' (*garibi*) can be removed. These hopes are not only economic but also social and political—people have an awareness of rights and their entitlements as citizens. Two questions emerge: Why is India poor and divided? And: Why do people continue to hope?

Chapter 2
Colonial India: impoverishment

The first question—regarding why India is poor and divided—is best split into three subsidiary questions. First, why is India poor? The underlying assumption that needs to be challenged here is that India is somehow inevitably a place of poverty and hardship. Second, why is India marked so strongly as a Hindu country? In this case there is a need to counter a tendency for people to imagine that India is—and has been for time immemorial—a country characterized by a religion called 'Hinduism'. Third, why are caste inequalities important in India? In this case it is necessary to challenge the common assumption, especially outside India, that India is and always has been riven by caste.

Economic impoverishment

India is difficult to define. The Ancient Persians used the term *Hindu*—and the Ancient Greeks used *Indoi*—to describe the people of the Indus River or, in other accounts, the people living 'beyond the Indus'. But 'India' and related words are fluid and somewhat indeterminate. By the time that medieval Europeans first began their sea voyages to 'the East' in the 16th century, the terms 'India' and 'Indies' referred to anywhere from the Cape of Africa to Indonesia. It was only in the 19th century that the British came to imagine 'India' in the terms in which it was understood up until its establishment in 1947 as an independent nation: as comprised of most of present-day

Myanmar, Bangladesh, India, and Pakistan—with Afghanistan and Nepal representing a kind of frontier.

India in this sense, and with respect to its current post-Independence boundaries, is a fertile country with rich alluvial soils, vast plains, reasonable water supplies, extensive mineral wealth (especially coal, iron, and manganese), and a long coastline providing excellent trading opportunities. One might therefore assume that the subcontinent would be rich. Indeed, it has been wealthy historically (Figure 1).

Europeans travelling in India in the 17th and 18th centuries stressed this aspect of India. The French traveller Bernier, having visited Bengal in about 1660, wrote of a region 'Richer than Egypt. It exports in abundance cottons and silks, rice, sugar and butter. It produces amply for its own consumption of wheat, vegetables, grains, fowls, ducks and geese.' In 1757 Lord Clive on entering

1. Humayun's Tomb, Delhi.

Murshidabad, the old capital of Bengal, enthused about a city 'As extensive, populous and rich as the city of London'. Even allowing for exaggeration and the point that visitors tended to meet elites, this evidence is useful. Indeed, according to one historian, India and China have been the richest parts of the world during eighteen of the past twenty centuries. The ubiquity of poverty in contemporary India thus needs to be explained with reference to colonial history rather than imagined as somehow an inevitable feature of the subcontinent.

In the 16th and 17th centuries improvements in ocean-going technology and navigation, combined with the increased wealth of western European countries, led to a series of European expeditions eastwards. They were seeking a less expensive means of acquiring spices and other commodities from the East than the overland route. A period of intense competition followed as the Portuguese, Spanish, Dutch, French, and English competed over access to trade routes to India.

The subsequent advance of European powers, especially the British, in India reflected weaknesses in the Mughal system of rule. The 'Mughals' had entered India in 1526. The first Emperor, Babur (1483–1530), and his descendants presided over a successful empire, which reached its zenith in 1707 and lasted, at least formally, until 1847. By the end of the reign of the Sixth Emperor Aurangzeb (1618–1707), who ruled from 1658 to 1707, the Mughal Empire covered two-thirds of the Indian subcontinent. The Mughal contribution to Indian culture is particularly notable, and Emperor Akbar (1556–1603) was an especially energetic patron of the arts, sponsoring intricate architecture, textile design, portraiture, and line drawing. Among the legacies of the Mughal Empire was also one of the icons of India: the Taj Mahal, built by the Emperor Shah Jahan from 1632.

The emperors had sought to centralize power through investing in infrastructure, bolstering agriculture, and engaging in political ritual, which achieved its highest form in the imperial *durbars*—large-scale public events in which people received an audience with the Emperor. But the Mughals depended in practice on the allegiance of numerous semi-autonomous princes or '*nawabs*'—an Urdu word meaning 'deputy'. By the later 17th century the loyalty of nawabs could not be assumed. At that time, the Mughals were compelled to counter wars and rebellion in many regions. These included a revolt in modern-day Afghanistan in 1672, a peasant rebellion near Delhi in the 1670s, and a protracted conflict in the 1660s with the Marathas, led by the charismatic warlord Chhatrapati Shivaji, who became a powerful symbol in the Indian Independence movement and Hindu nationalist circles (Figure 2). In the 18th century, many of the provincial elites began resisting paying for expensive wars. By the 1740s, for example, the provincial governors in the regions of Bengal, Awadh, and the Deccan transformed themselves from dependants of the Mughals to independent rulers.

Mughal difficulties in governing their territory allowed European powers to become increasingly active in the Indian subcontinent. During the 17th and 18th centuries, the English established their supremacy in relation to other European countries in India, partly reflecting their naval strength. In particular, the English managed to outmanoeuvre the French in the third quarter of the 18th century.

It is broadly possible to identify three phases in the imperial dominance of the English (or British as they became after the union in 1707) in India. During the first phase, lasting from 1600 until 1757, the English charged the responsibility of engaging with India to the East India Company (or 'The Company'), a joint stock company established in London in 1600, whose focus during most of this first period was trade. Under its Royal Charter, the Company was granted a monopoly over Eastern trade, and through the 17th century it established trading posts in Surat, Madras, Bombay, and Calcutta within the subcontinent.

2. A statue of Chhatrapati Shivaji of Maharashtra.

For the first thirteen years of the Company's existence, English merchants and aristocrats financed individual voyages to the East on a joint stock basis, each becoming shareholders in standalone trips by English vessels. From 1613, however, stocks were invested in the establishment of a fleet each year over a period of four years. This allowed the Company to plan over a longer period and eliminated rivalry between voyages. This, in turn, created larger profits.

From 1670 the English Crown gave the Company the right to develop an army, build fortresses, mint money, and make territorial acquisitions. But it was not until the 18th century, reflecting rivalry with the French East India Company and the waning of Mughal power, that the Company became heavily involved in expanding its power politically. The Battle of Plassey in 1757 and Battle of Buxar in 1764 were two especially decisive victories for the Company that gave it—and Britain—control over Bengal. This period of expansion in the mid- to late 18th century consolidated the 'Presidencies' of Bengal, Madras, and Bombay, which functioned as sovereign territories of the Company. During this second phase, the Company's army grew rapidly, too, from 3,000 in 1750 to 155,000 in 1805, and, unlike their Mughal counterparts, the Company's army received dedicated training, pay, and a pension. Reflecting the size and professionalism of its fighting force, the Company expanded territorially, first in the east and south and then in the north.

This expansion sometimes occurred via outright victory. But it also involved compromise and accommodation. Where the Company found a local ruler difficult to subdue—or where the rewards did not justify a battle—the British made treaties that left the leader in power but as a dependant of the Company. The Indian rulers of these regions—what became known as the 'Princely States'—acknowledged British overlordship in return for some political autonomy. The extent of British-held territory in India in 1856 is shown in Figure 3.

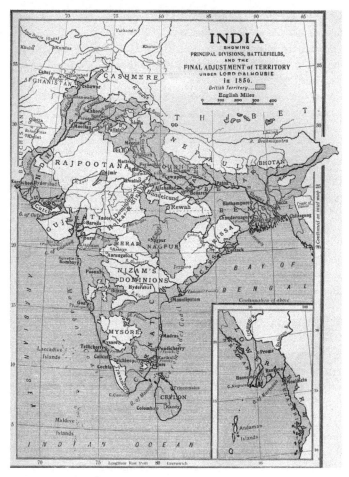

3. Map of India 1856.

During this second phase, the ruinous impact of British imperialism began to become apparent. The Company exploited the Indian countryside through levying tax demands, which were much higher than was typical under the Mughals. It also increased these demands over time. For example, in 1765–6 the British realized land revenue from Bengal of roughly £1.5 million. By 1771–2 this figure had risen to £2.3 million, and by 1775–6 to £2.8 million. The Company's profits in Bengal rose from £3 million in 1765 to £22 million by 1818. The effects of this system on the local population were dire. Even the Company's own official report of 1770 referred to the 'ruinous condition' of rural Bengal. In the same year, 10 million Bengalis—a third of the population—succumbed to famine.

Indians hugely outnumbered the British in the subcontinent. Partly as a consequence, and reflecting also prior Mughal arrangements, the British relied heavily on local agents to administer the countryside, usually people with a measure of authority and often larger landowners. This arrangement not only provided the institutional architecture for the appropriation of India's agricultural profits, it also had the effect of further dividing rural areas socially between relatively wealthy local landowners and the comparatively poor.

In 1793, Lord Cornwallis, the Governor General of British India, created a land system in Bengal that identified a set of Indian landowners, known locally as 'zamindars', to be partners in the extraction of profit from agriculture. Through the zamindari system of agricultural taxation, the Company created a set of local notables who could act as representatives of the British. Under the Permanent Settlement of 1793, the British agreed to tax Bengali zamindars at a fixed rate. Zamindars would in turn extract rents from tenant farmers and peasants. The Permanent Settlement also restricted the coercive powers of zamindars, limiting their role to revenue collection. As the historian Ranajit Guha has argued, the British Permanent Settlement reflected imperialists' belief in the importance of creating a class of 'improving landlords', who they assumed would manage the land in a fair and productive manner. The British believed that preventing coercion and fixing the tax rate would prevent zamindars from extracting so much rent as to undermine long-term agricultural productivity. They also believed that zamindars would improve agricultural production over time in order to increase their income as intermediaries. Land taxes, however, were higher than those in England and the inflexibility of their enforcement, even during times of natural disaster, resulted in the bankruptcy of many landlords and periodic famines.

Elsewhere in India, including throughout much of the Bombay and Madras Presidencies, a 'ryotwari' system prevailed, in which peasants ('ryots') paid land tax directly to the Company, without a zamindar intermediary. Here, too, the system proved exploitative and in many cases created hardship. The British requirement that ryots pay in cash increased small landowners' dependence on moneylenders, prevented them from investing in the development of their landholdings, and increased their vulnerability to drought and other catastrophes.

A third phase of British economic exploitation of India can be traced to the first three decades of the 19th century and involved the emergence of a more systematic form of imperial economic exploitation. By the late 18th and early 19th centuries, the writings of Adam Smith, particularly in his book *The Wealth of Nations* (1776), had captured the imagination of leading thinkers and industrialists in Britain. They began to challenge the monopoly of the Company and called for India to be opened up for free trade. Specifically, leading manufacturers demanded the right to sell products to the Indian market. From 1813 onwards, the promotion of free trade effectively became a cover for the British to twist their relationship with India to fit a classic colonial model. The British promoted the outflow of raw materials from the 'periphery' (India) to a wealthy 'core' (Britain) that in turn marketed manufactured goods back in south Asia. Indian manufactured goods were subject to high entry tariffs, making it very difficult for any Indian entrepreneur to sell to Britain. At the same time, there were effectively no tariffs on British manufactured goods entering India. The results were dramatic. The sale of British cotton and yarn increased tenfold in India between 1813 and 1833. At the same time, the value of manufactured cotton goods exported from India fell from £1.3 million in 1815 to £100,000 in 1832.

As a country reliant on the export of primary commodities, India was exposed to the vagaries of the global market. The Indian economy suffered a major depression in the 1820s, when a surplus of indigo and cotton combined with declining European demand, and another severe economic shock in the 1840s. Across the 19th century there was a rapid increase in the frequency and severity of famine. Between 1876 and 1878 in south India a severe drought, exacerbated by the commercialization of agriculture and free market policies, led to the deaths of an estimated 5.5 million people from starvation—approximately 18 per cent of the Madras Presidency at the time—in what became known as the 'Great Famine'. Rudyard Kipling's short story *William the Conqueror* neatly conveys imperial assumptions about the role of the British in India with regard to managing the famine.

Indian industry also suffered. As late as 1800 the most developed parts of India were on a par with the most developed parts of Britain in terms of the economic situation of the masses. Methods of production and of industrial and commercial organization were also similar to those extant in most parts of Europe. Christopher Bayly's account of India's thriving local and regional market economy during the 18th century provides rich evidence of India's relatively robust economic situation prior to the main phase of British imperialism. But the import of cheap, machine-produced goods into India in the 19th century undermined traditional artisanal industry. Ironically, the handloom industry in India—which had partly drawn Europeans to India in the 17th century—collapsed. The old handloom industry was in dire straits in Britain, too, but there a new machine industry replaced old craft. In India there was no such technological development.

Many traditional craft workers moved from urban areas to the Indian countryside. Thriving manufacturing towns emptied over the space of a generation. According to one report, the population of Dacca in Bengal declined from 150,000 to around 35,000 between about 1815 and 1840. Urban-rural migration in turn placed more pressure on the agricultural sector. Other victims of deindustrialization migrated to other British colonies to work in plantations, often becoming indentured labourers.

This system of economic exploitation required the British to stymie new industry in India. Indian businesspeople interested in developing industry faced stiff opposition from British capitalists, who had better access to technology, infrastructure, and credit.

Environmental destruction accompanied this exploitation, especially from the early 19th century onwards. The British encouraged landlords to convert forests into cultivable land to enhance revenue. They also placed heavy demand on Indian timber, especially *sal*, *deodar*, and *teak*, used to make railway sleepers. The British vigorously promoted the planting of trees that had an immediate commercial utility and thereby reduced the area under mixed forests. When demand for timber increased in the 1870s, the British enacted a Forest Act in 1878, which effectively allowed them to commandeer forests that had formerly been managed by communities. These dynamics had particularly devastating implications for so-called 'tribal' populations who predominated in areas of India with copious forests.

British exploitation via unequal trade was superimposed upon the previous system of revenue extraction rather than replacing it. The British continued to remove millions of pounds of 'tribute' from India, particularly through 'home charges': a term referring to the putative costs—vastly inflated by the British—of governing India. The amount remitted from India to Britain between 1851 and 1901 increased sevenfold and the export of treasure (especially gold) from India to Britain continued to rise rapidly in the early decades of the 20th century. In addition, British financiers engaged in speculative investment in India, especially from the last quarter of the 19th century onwards, accruing vast profits.

These points help to contextualize the struggles of the rural poor in India in the 21st century—people such as Minu and Afrozi. The British paid scant attention to the plight of rural denizens of India and, when they did so, tended to adopt a patronizing approach. They reinforced local social and economic hierarchies that separated the larger landowners from the labouring classes.

It is important to enter two caveats with respect to the British 'impoverishment' of India, however. First, some historians emphasize Britain's positive contribution to India via infrastructural and institutional development. The British introduction of the telegraph in India from the 1850s onwards greatly enhanced communication. The British also improved the infrastructure in India in the second half of the 19th century through the construction of railways, roads, canals, and irrigation. By 1880, 9,000 miles of railway had been laid in India, and by 1920 this figure had reached 38,000 miles. Better irrigation and rail transport transformed opportunities for agricultural production, increasing agricultural output.

British rule also contributed to infrastructural development through promoting the growth of Calcutta, Madras, and Bombay, which by 1850 were among the largest cities in the world. The British introduced a more systematic and developed system of law, Western property rights, newspapers, and forms of administrative order, including policing and the application of statistics to the process of governance. These initiatives assisted Indians in their struggle for independence and provided a foundation for India's post-colonial development.

In addition, and reflecting the influence of Jeremy Bentham's notion of utilitarianism and associated emphasis on the importance of science and reason, the British focused on how to 'improve' the Indian population, particularly through education. The imperialists devalued Indian knowledge, in line with the view of Thomas Macaulay (1800–59), a member of the Governor General's Council, that 'a single shelf of a good European library [is] worth the whole native literature of India and Arabia'. But the British educational drive did lead to the establishment of a number of schools and colleges, including institutions that were not simply imitators of Western practice. One of the most important benefits of British colonialism in India was arguably the spread of the English language, for example via English-medium schools. Knowledge of English helped to knit Indian elites into a wider world system in the 20th century.

A few powerful Indian industrialists also emerged in the later 19th century, often out of the trading merchant or banking classes and in the larger cities such as Bombay (now known as Mumbai), Ahmedabad, Cawnpore (now Kanpur), and Calcutta (now Kolkata). Such successful businessmen included the Tatas, who became prominent in the running of cotton mills in the 1860s, and the Birlas, who were wealthy traders in cotton and jute, and then became involved in the running of cotton and jute mills in the early 20th century. It also included the rise of Indian companies involved in the processing of agricultural commodities, such as sugar corporations.

Thus a type of 'modernity' surfaced in India in the later 19th century. This was associated with the infrastructural, technological, and educational advances pushed forward by the British and also reflected what Christopher Bayly referred to as a 'critical and entrepreneurial spirit' among Indian elites.

But it was a modernity that primarily benefited the British within India and a minority of wealthy Indians. The gains provided by the imperialists were mainly geared to increasing British profits and security rather than encouraging Indian capitalism or broad-based social development. For example, the pattern and functioning of the railways reflected the commercial interests of the British. British-run schools sought not to develop the capabilities of the masses but to create a cadre of Indians who could assist in administering India.

Moreover, the British controlled most of the modern industry that existed in India in the 19th century and early 20th century. They discouraged enterprise that might engender India's growth, for example in the area of power generation. The Indian businesspeople tended to be junior partners in enterprises with the British and focused either on trade, banking, or agricultural processing.

The main point therefore remains. The British transformed India from a country with a mixed agricultural and industrial economy, into an agricultural colony of British manufacturing capitalism. In 1800 western Europe and the seaboard of North America had twice the GDP per capita of India; by 1900 those regions had ten times the Indian figure.

The nationalist movement

A more important rejoinder to the narrative regarding Britain's impoverishment of India focuses on the nationalist response to imperialism. To appreciate the context of this Indian nationalism, it is necessary to emphasize that economic exploitation under the British was bound up with a loss of political sovereignty. In the context of fears over misdemeanours within the East India Company, the British Parliament passed a 'Regulating Act' in 1773, which stipulated that a Governor General would rule British territory in India, answerable to the British Crown. It also elevated Warren Hastings, the Governor of Bengal, to the status of Governor General of Bengal and brought the Madras and Bombay Presidencies under his control. In addition, it established a Supreme Court of Justice in Calcutta, with a jurisdiction over

Company servants. The Act provided the Company with a centralized system of administration in India that was, at least nominally, bound by British law.

The British intervened more decisively in the political governance of the Indian subcontinent in the mid-19th century. Concerned about growing resistance to imperial rule, the British passed a Government of India Act of 1858 which abolished the Company's rule and created the office of the Secretary of State for India to superintend the affairs of India, advised by a new Council of India with fifteen members, based in London. The Governor General, appointed by the Crown, became known as the Viceroy. The fiction of the British government being at arm's length from the management of India was thereby ended.

The colonial state enlarged and restructured the Indian army in the middle years of the 19th century. It also made moves to map and chronicle the population over which it ruled. From 1871, the British government undertook decadal censuses of the Indian population. The academic discipline of anthropology emerged to acquire information about 'Indian cultures'.

To be sure, the British made periodic attempts to grant greater political autonomy to Indians. These various changes provided a growing degree of regional political participation for Indians while also ensuring that power remained centralized within the hands of the British. The Indian Councils Act of 1861 created 'parochial councils' in Bengal, Madras, and Bombay. British officials presided over these councils but were mandated to consult with Indian non-officials. The Indian Councils Act of 1892 expanded these councils and allowed some Indian authorities to make recommendations on the appointment of council members. Reforms in the first two decades of the 20th century went markedly further. Indeed, in 1917 the British made a Declaration promising 'the progressive realisation of responsible government in India as an integral part of the empire'. New measures divested greater power to Indian-controlled regional councils. But all of these moves had little effect on the Indian population at large. The British, at the centre, continued to control key aspects of government. Indeed, shooting, imprisonment, arbitrary violence, and restrictive legislation became increasingly apparent during the late 19th and especially the 20th century. The period between 1750 and 1947 was one of gradual but dramatic seizure of power by the British over India, and it was the combination of economic and political disempowerment that seeded Indian nationalism.

During the 19th century, the Indian population made increasing attempts to wrest back some degree of economic power and political sovereignty from the British. There were food riots in the city of Madras (now Chennai) as early as 1806. There were also peasant rebellions against land taxes in the 1830s in north India. Moreover, the colonial state's forcible seizure of forested land generated widespread tension and occasional revolt. For example, many Santals in present-day Jharkhand moved from being successful hunter-gatherers to bonded labourers. Furious at colonial economic and local political exploitation, sections of this community fought the British in 1855. Historians estimate that 15,000 Santals died in the British push to restore control.

A more significant revolt began in 1857 in Meerut, located in what is now western Uttar Pradesh. Indian soldiers were angry that the British had purportedly greased rifle cartridges—which soldiers had to bite—with pig or beef fat, repugnant to Muslims and Hindus respectively. The incident connected with disgruntlement among soldiers about their working conditions and pay. On the night of 10 May 1857 a section of the Native Cavalry mutinied in Meerut. The so-called 'Indian Munity' or 'Great Revolt' in Meerut soon spread to Delhi. An almost autonomous revolt occurred roughly simultaneously in Awadh, where small landowners and artisans laid siege to the British in Lucknow. Yet another centre of rebellion emerged in central India where under the leadership of the Rani (Queen) of Jhansi disenchanted peasants rose up against the British. In all these cases, grievances were partly economic, connected to the high level of British land revenue demands, and partly social, related to anger at British racial arrogance. The British were able to put down the revolts of 1857–8, although the battles were often bloody and protracted.

At roughly this time more narrowly intellectual critiques of Britain's effect on the Indian economy began to circulate. One of the most notable came from the Parsi thinker Dadabhai Naoroji (1825–1917). Naoroji argued that the British contributed to India's impoverishment by suppressing Indian industry, instituting exploitative land taxation laws, and using revenue collected from India to finance the British-run bureaucracy and wars. Naoroji also argued that high-paying jobs in business and the civil service in India almost exclusively went to foreign personnel, who took their fortunes home with them rather than investing in India. He concluded that the British were draining out wealth from India to Britain. Naoroji believed in the fundamental fairness of the British, but felt that this was being subverted in the case of India; his book was titled *Poverty and Un-British Rule in India*.

Such critiques became more common in the last third of the 19th century in association with the rise of an elite Indian 'civil society'. The growth of Indian civic action was manifest in a sharp rise in the production of newspapers, greater legal activity among Indians, and efforts to improve public education, including for girls. In addition, Western-educated Indians established political associations aimed at reflecting on how Indians could improve their relationship to the colonial power, most notably the Indian National Congress, established in 1885. Not especially radical at its inception, the Indian National Congress became a major engine of the nationalist movement in the following century. In the late 19th century and early 20th century, Indian women became more assertive politically, first around patriarchal ideas about women's roles and later with reference to British imperialism and through organizations such as the Arya Mahila Samaj, established in 1882 by the reformer and education activist Pandita Ramabai (1858–1922).

The Indian National Congress—or 'Congress'—became actively involved in protest against the British in the first decade of the 20th century. In 1905 Lord Curzon divided the province of Bengal into two separate regions in order to reduce nationalist activity. In response Congress leaders boycotted British goods, emphasizing instead 'swadeshi' (self-provisioning) and the need to rebuild indigenous industry.

But it was not until the second decade of the 20th century that the nationalist movement became a popular struggle, in part reflecting the work of M. K. Gandhi. Mohandas Gandhi, now known widely as 'Mahatma' Gandhi (Mahatma means 'great soul'), was born and raised in Gujarat in a Hindu merchant caste family. After training as a lawyer in London's Inner Temple he practised law in South Africa. As a young man he became involved in the struggle of the expatriate Indian community for civil rights in South Africa. He also experimented with non-violent civil disobedience as a means of opposition to the state and wrote a critique of British rule in India: *Hind Swaraj* (1908).

Gandhi returned to India in 1915. Appalled by the deprivation he encountered in rural areas, he set about protesting against excessive land taxation and the political disempowerment of the poor. In his first few years in India, however, Gandhi was not concerned with pushing for freedom from the British. Rather, as the historian Faisal Devji has shown in a book on the Mahatma, he wanted a type of 'liberal imperial order'. Empire in this vision would be founded on the philosophies and life practices of the oppressed of the world and consist of a collection of self-governing units, equal in status and allowing the free flow of people between different nations. In this configuration, Gandhi imagined ultimate authority residing not with the state but in the individual.

Yet Gandhi came to focus more clearly on the need to expel the British from India. Gandhi's political skill in this area had three key dimensions. First, he forged a bond with his followers through his own personal appearance and lifestyle. He had few possessions, wore a simple *dhoti* and shawl, and ate simple vegetarian food. The body—and Gandhi's own body—became a visible marker that could connect political issues to people's everyday concerns over food and nutrition. Second, he provided a vocabulary that could inform and orient aspects of the Independence movement. Gandhi emphasized three core principles: *swaraj* (self-rule), *swadeshi* (self-provisioning or self-sufficiency), and *satyagraha*, which literally means 'truth force' but tended to refer to a form of non-violent civil disobedience that he had developed in South Africa: sit-ins, road blocks, and hunger strikes, for example. The emphasis on non-violence was especially important in shifting the moral argument in India such that 'ordinary Indians', rather than the British, came to stand for justice and fairness. Third, one of Gandhi's major strengths was this capacity to appeal to people over and above particularistic interests based on caste affiliation or faith.

The First World War exacerbated Indians' fears over economic and political exploitation and was the immediate context for some of Gandhi's first nationwide protests in India. Sixty thousand Indians lost their lives in the First World War, and many Indians resented these losses. Taxes were increased to fund the war effort, and military spending resulted in inflation throughout India, with particularly damaging effects on the countryside. Moreover, shortly after the end of the war—on 13 April 1919—Indian and Nepali soldiers, commanded by the British military officer General Dyer, killed at least 379 people and injured more than 1,200 who had gathered peacefully for a fair in Jallianwala Bagh in the north Indian city of Amritsar.

For many who had remained agnostic about Indian nationalism, the Jallianwala Bagh massacre was a watershed. The Bengali poet and Nobel Prize winner Rabindranath Tagore renounced his knighthood. In a move with long-term significance for India, the hitherto pro-British family of the prominent Indian lawyer Motilal Nehru began to protest against colonial rule. Over the next two decades Motilal's son, Jawaharlal Nehru, developed a socialist critique of British rule that emphasized a need to nationalize industry and protect the poor. Nehru became a key leader in the Congress.

In response to this growing discontent among Indians, and as leader of the Congress from 1921 onwards, Gandhi expanded his non-violent campaigns. These typically connected economic discontent to a wide range of other issues, including women's rights, an end to the practice of caste untouchability, and a desire for self-rule. Between 1920 and 1922, movements focused on non-cooperation, including strikes, boycotts, and rallies, marked urban India. In a powerful expression of the *swadeshi* principle, Gandhi and his supporters enjoined people to abandon Western cloth, British schools, British law courts, and British honours and titles.

Congress was often split on the question of the extent to which all protests should be non-violent. Gandhi, though highly influential, had opponents. It is particularly important to recognize the existence of a socialist, radical wing within the nationalist movement. Historians often discuss this wing with reference to Bhagat Singh, a charismatic Indian revolutionary executed by the British with two other revolutionaries in 1931 for murdering a British police officer.

The Global Depression of the 1930s led the British to protect British industry, which in turn triggered a collapse in the prices that Indian producers obtained for key exports. Between 1929 and 1932 the prices of India's major cash crops more than halved. This also provoked a credit crisis, as moneylenders were unable to recover interest from peasant debtors.

Reflecting the deteriorating economic situation and concern over the failure of the British to grant Indians self-rule, Gandhi decided to protest against unreasonable British taxes on the Indian production of salt. The British were dismissive. One official remarked that he would not lie awake at night worrying about salt. But Gandhi's focus was inspired: not only was salt itself important economically—the salt tax represented 8.2 per cent of the British Raj tax revenue—but it also had a crucial symbolic importance as a basic need of people living (and sweating) in a tropical climate. 'Next to air and water, salt is perhaps the greatest necessity of life,' Gandhi said. The Mahatma walked for 241 miles to make salt on the Gujarati coast (Figure 4).

The Salt March involved greater numbers of women than any previous oppositional movement. It also inaugurated a wave of civil disobedience in India, including the non-payment of taxes,

4. Mohandas Karamchand Gandhi, political and spiritual leader, on the Salt March, 1930.

strikes, the barricading of liquor outlets, and protests against British restrictions on the use of forests. In some instances, the British found themselves facing mass civil unrest. By 1933, the British had jailed about 135,000 Indians, including roughly 5,000 women.

During the 1930s, the British government responded to the growing and coordinated opposition to the Raj through further institutional reform, most notably in passing the Government of India Act (1935). This increased the number of voters in India to 35 million and transferred control of law and order issues to provincial legislatures managed by Indians. But the Act continued the pattern of providing some provincial autonomy while ensuring that the centre (under the British) remained in control of key areas of decision-making, notably defence and foreign affairs. The Act did little to satisfy Indian nationalists.

During the Second World War the British appropriated enormous amounts of food and other resources from India, and the food shortage led to soaring prices. It is estimated that between 3.5 million and 3.8 million people died in the resulting famine in Bengal. The Quit India movement that began in 1942 was the most violent of the civil disobedience campaigns. Protesters destroyed hundreds of government buildings, and the British did not quash the uprisings until spring 1943. Yet another movement occurred in late 1945 and early 1946, this time on the issue of British treatment of soldiers who had participated in Indian nationalist Subhas Chandra Bose's doomed effort at mustering an Indian National Army to counter the British during the war. Facing problems at home, the British sent out a mission in spring 1946 to discuss the terms of Indian Independence.

In sum, the British exploited India economically and wrested political control of the region for themselves. But Indian nationalists challenged this settlement, ultimately winning self-rule. In the process they developed institutional forms and experience that were crucial to the making of India in the 20th and 21st centuries. This story partly explains the frustration of Prempal and it helps to contextualize the experience of Minu and Afrozi.

Chapter 3
Colonial India: religious and caste divides

Hinduism and partition

In the popular imagination India is often identified as a Hindu country. This is connected to the increased confidence of many Hindus inside India. But the 'Hindu-ness' of India and the strength of religious divides and inequalities that are associated with this Hindu-ness need to be explained historically rather than assumed as an aspect of Indian culture.

There are multiple problems with the proposition that India is essentially a Hindu country. There are many religions in India and also some who do not follow any faith. Buddhism and Jainism arose in India in approximately the 5th century BCE, in part as rationalist reactions against the more superstitious aspects of the Vedic tradition associated with Hinduism. Buddhism spread throughout the subcontinent as the preferred religion of the commercial classes and was ultimately adopted by the Maurya Emperor Ashoka in the 3rd century BCE. It remained a dominant religion on the subcontinent until around the time of the Gupta Empire (c.320 to 650 CE) (see Figure 5). Islam has also been crucially important in India's history. As early as the 8th century, Muslims occupied portions of north-west India, and their social and political influence grew rapidly during the following millennium, partly as a result of the arrival of traders on the west coast

5. The Great Stupa, 2nd century BC, Sanchi, India.

from Arabia. There are also long-established Sikh, Jain, Zoroastrian, Jewish, and Christian communities in India, often religious populations that are concentrated in specific regions—for example Sikhs in the north-west and Christians in the south and north-east.

Another objection to the notion that India is Hindu would focus on the difficulty of identifying a singular 'Hinduism' in the subcontinent. The religion that is now termed Hinduism cohered only relatively recently in India's history.

Various qualifications are necessary, however, in making this argument about the fuzziness or even 'incoherence' of Hinduism. The holy scriptures (the Vedas), written in the period between 1500 and 500 BCE, gave form to customary practices, and there were periods in India's pre-modern history where aspects of Hinduism achieved a relatively intelligible overall shape, notably between 500 BCE and 300 BCE when several Hindu schools of philosophy were founded and universities, monasteries, and temples built. There are key Hindu texts that have informed religious practice across a wide area including the epics, the *Mahabharata*, which describes the mythological wars between the Kauravas and Pandavas, and the *Ramayana*, which details the journey of Prince Ram to rescue his wife Sita from the demon king Ravana. The *Bhagavad Gita*, in which Lord Krishna instructs the warrior prince Arjun to perform his duty without concern for reward, forms a crucial section of the *Mahabharata* and is considered a synthesis of many religious traditions. These texts were composed in Sanskrit, the lingua franca throughout much of ancient south Asia, which was heavily influenced by the Aryans and is the root language of most north Indian languages.

It is true too that some beliefs transcend regional differences lending logic to notions of a composite 'Hinduism'. These beliefs include a sense of the importance of key aims of life (also called *purusarthas*): *dharma* (ethics/duty), *artha* (prosperity/work), *kama* (desires/passion), and *moksha* (liberation/freedom). They included, too, a belief in *karma*, which refers to the relationship between action and consequences of that action; *samsara*, which refers to the cycle of rebirth (and hence reincarnation); *yoga*, which are paths or practices intended to provide health and spiritual enlightenment; and *ahimsa* (non-violence). Another prominent belief among some Hindus is the notion that life is divided into four stages or '*asharmas*': *Brahmacharya* (student), *Grihastha* (householder), *Vanaprastha* (retirement and advisory role), and *Sannyasa* (renunciation). But for all these provisos—regarding textual reference points, prior synthesis, and shared beliefs—what was labelled 'Hinduism' when the British ruled over India in the 18th and early 19th centuries was in truth a wide array of shamanistic practices, customs, and rites that reflected the specific histories of different local social groups.

'Hindu', then, was a label applied by Europeans in part under the mistaken belief that the religious practices they were witnessing had a tightly organized structure analogous to Christianity.

A panoply of practices, including Buddhism, devotional cults, and animism, were parcelled together and referred to as 'Hindu'/ 'Hindoo'. Edward Said has argued that colonial powers shore up their own sense of being moral, rational, and civilized through denigrating the cultures they encountered as immoral, irrational, and uncivilized. The British disparaged Hinduism as fantastical, exotic, and mystical.

Indian religious leaders reacted energetically to this colonial vision of Hinduism. On the one hand, they often appropriated the idea that there is a coherent religion called Hinduism bound together through various animating ideas, and they built on this notion to develop public rituals. On the other hand, they reacted against the idea of Hinduism as mystical and irrational, and did so sometimes through reforming religious practice.

Among the most prominent of these Hindu leaders in the 19th century was the Bengali intellectual Swami Vivekananda (1863–1902). Vivekananda argued that Hinduism was a world religion in a way that resonated with the imperial imagination. Yet he challenged other aspects of the colonial construction of Hinduism, emphasizing Hinduism's contribution to an understanding of tolerance, while also calling on Hindus to engage in a programme of 'self-strengthening' and 'social service'. Vivekananda argued that Hinduism should do away with its fixation on ceremony and instead focus on enriching people's lives, offering service to the poor, and stressing its connections to notions of peace and spirituality. In his journeys to Europe and America in the 1890s, Vivekananda was a charismatic ambassador for the religion he represented, crucial in raising awareness of Hinduism outside India and cementing the notion that Hinduism has a special relationship to ideas of acceptance. In his speech in Chicago in 1893, Vivekananda averred: 'We believe not only in universal toleration, but we accept all religions as true. I am proud to belong to a nation which has sheltered the persecuted and the refugees of all religions and all nations of the earth.'

In another instance of appropriation, Swami Dayanand (1824–83), a scholar of the Sanskrit language, founded the Arya Samaj movement in Punjab in 1875. Dayanand absorbed the critiques of Christian missionaries regarding the treatment of widows in Hinduism as well as colonial critiques of caste. But Dayanand argued that a revived Hinduism based on the Vedas could best address pernicious 'customs'. Dayanand also argued that Hinduism is the true ancient religion of all humankind, achieving its most perfect expression in the subcontinent. The Arya Samaj quickly attracted the support of upwardly mobile commercial classes and rich peasants in Punjab.

According to the anthropologist Chris Fuller, the first major attempt to create a politicized Hindu ritual was the invention of the public Ganesha Chaturthi yearly festival in Maharashtra in the 1890s by Bal Gangadhar Tilak, a member of the Indian National Congress. Certainly the following fifty years were to see the rise of multiple efforts to develop Hindu nationalism, which often had a 'revivalist' tone. Vinayak Damodar Savarkar (1883–1966) was especially influential in laying out a vision of India as a Hindu country that needs to be defended against foreign invasion from those professing other faiths and purged of alien elements. Savarkar emphasized a common bond between Hindus, Sikhs, Buddhists, and Jains, stressing that they all dwelt within and paid homage to 'India' as a type of motherland. Savarkar's teachings in turn influenced the Rashtriya Swayamsevak Sangh (RSS), founded in 1925 by Keshav Hedgewar (1884–1940), an erstwhile member of the Congress from Maharashtra. Under Hedgewar the RSS provided cultural, sporting, and military-style organizational structures in which Indian young men engaged in the perfection of the male body—a response to colonial constructions of the Hindu body as 'effeminate' or 'effete'. By 1947 the RSS had half a million members.

The rise of assertive Hindu leaders, interacting with the British emphasis on people's membership of distinct religions, also encouraged Muslims to develop a clearer national consciousness.

Notably, Sir Syed Ahmed Khan (1817–98) developed the Aligarh Movement in which he urged supporters to embrace Western education. Khan also founded the Aligarh Anglo-Muhammadan Oriental College as an institutional base for his mission.

The Aligarh movement, in turn, influenced Indian nationalism and—ultimately—the shape of independent India itself. Senior Muslims associated with Khan, who felt alienated from the Congress, established a separate All-India Muslim League (known later simply as the Muslim League) in Dacca in 1906. Its original goal was to protect the particular rights of Muslims in India as a bulwark against Congress. Under the Western-educated former barrister Muhammad Ali Jinnah (1876–1948), who led the Muslim League between 1916 and 1947, the League focused especially on the issue of Muslims' representation within a future independent India.

During the 19th century the idea had arisen within elite Muslim circles that Muslims and Hindus constituted distinct nations—so different were their habits, practices, and ideals. This 'two nation theory' gained traction in the 1930s, most prominently at first through the poet Muhammad Iqbal, who argued that Muslims required a separate state within India in order to live securely in the subcontinent. Chaudhri Rahmat Ali, a student, responded by inventing the word 'Pakistan', which means 'land of the pure' but is also an acronym of Punjab (P), Afghan (A), Kashmir (K), Sind (S), and 'tan' possibly referring to Baluchistan—all regions in the north-west of India.

The Government of India Act of 1935 increased Muslims' fears of Hindu domination because it conferred power on Indian legislatures controlled by Hindus. In an address to the Muslim League in Lahore in March 1940, Jinnah stated that the north-western and eastern regions of India in which Muslims dominated numerically should constitute distinct states with considerable autonomy and only a weak federal government having legislative control over each.

This idea proved important in discussions over the shape of post-imperial India. After announcing the timelines for their withdrawal from India, the British government appointed Lord Louis Mountbatten as Viceroy in March 1947 to oversee the transition. In the ensuing discussions, Nehru and Jinnah could not reach agreement on the question of whether a united India should have a strong or weak central government. Jinnah preferred to see India divided rather than a united India with a strong Hindu-dominated central government. Partition became the compromise position of sorts. In June 1947, Mountbatten announced that Bengal and Punjab would be divided along religious lines. The deadline for British withdrawal was brought forward to 15 August to ensure that the fragile interim governments would not break down, allowing just ten weeks to formalize the two new nations' borders, constitutions, and division of assets. India became two nations: the Republic of India and the Dominion of Pakistan—the latter of which was administratively divided between East Pakistan (now Bangladesh), and West Pakistan (now Pakistan) (Figure 6).

In Punjab, Partition was particularly violent. Its districts were not clearly divided along religious lines and Sikhs were distributed relatively evenly in both east and west. Sir Cyril Radcliffe, a judge, drew the boundary hastily, under great pressure from all sides. Basing the division purely on demographic composition proved controversial. Sikhs opposed the loss of Lahore to Pakistan, as the city had religious significance as the former capital of the Sikh Empire. Sikhs expelled non-Sikhs from land in the east, while Muslims did likewise in the west. This led to widespread violence. Approximately 100,000 women were abducted. Though the exact number of killings was not recorded, it is estimated to have been at least 200,000 and perhaps as many as 2 million. Partitioning Bengal was less violent. The border remained open well into the 1950s, and populations shifted in waves, as opposed to the sudden expulsions from the Punjab. Overall, it is estimated that 15 million people were displaced by Partition—the largest forced migration of the 20th century. It is noteworthy, however, that after Partition

6. **Citizens of Calcutta, India, climbing on lorries and tramcars celebrating Independence Day, 1947.**

approximately 35 million Muslims remained in India—10 per cent of the total population. The bloodshed and horror of Partition is movingly captured in Khushwant Singh's book *Train to Pakistan*.

In sum, India was not and is not wholly Hindu but encompasses great religious diversity. It became more Hindu in the period between 1800 and 1947 in the sense that the idea of 'being Hindu' became much stronger (as did the idea of 'being Muslim'). Indeed, 'Hinduism', through the work of figures such as Vivekananda and Savarkar, became a global religion alongside Christianity and Islam. Finally, it is important to note that the notion that India is/was Hindu is not only a proposition but also a 'myth' in Roland Barthes's sense: a system of beliefs that structures thought, politics, and public action—and continues to do so today. It is this mythologizing that partly explains the type of religious discrimination and exclusion that Afrozi encounters in contemporary western Uttar Pradesh.

Caste

Another assumption commonly made about India is that it is sharply divided by caste—an understandable observation in the context of the types of discrimination experienced by many low castes in India. But this assumption is problematic.

It is important to note first of all that there is no direct translation for 'caste' in India. The word caste is derived from the Portuguese word *casta* meaning 'pure breed'. 'Caste' in India is associated with several vernacular terms, among them the term *varna*, which means literally 'colour' in Sanskrit. The Vedas refer to four varnas: Brahmins, who were traditionally priests; Kshatriyas (warriors); Vaisyas (merchants); and Sudras, who performed other tasks, usually of a manual nature. The Brahmins, Kshatriyas, and Vaisyas together comprise the 'twice born' or 'Forward' castes; the Sudras being commonly termed the 'Backward' castes. So-called 'untouchables' lie outside the varna hierarchy altogether and were historically associated with degrading occupations. Those belonging to this category were regarded as 'untouchable' as their work was considered ritually polluting. They are unnamed in the Vedas—the term 'Dalit', which means 'oppressed' in Sanskrit, was used from the early 20th century onwards to signify their oppressed social status.

Each varna is comprised of thousands of *jatis* (which means 'species' or 'type') and refers to caste groups historically associated with particular occupations and each with their own notion of how they are placed with respect to the varna hierarchy. In India today jati is more important than varna in people's understandings of caste. Individual jatis often practise forms of arranged marriage wherein until recently they have not typically married outside their jati group. There is a variable regional geography to caste within India, for example there is a relatively high proportion of Sudras, and low proportion of Brahmins and Kshatriyas, in the south of the country, and individual jatis are often concentrated geographically within specific regions.

There was a great deal of writing on caste in India in the thirty years after Indian Independence in 1947 in part reflecting a European fascination with a social institution that did not exist 'at home'. Prominent was the French anthropologist Louis Dumont, who argued that the caste system is strongly hierarchical—his famous book was titled *Homo Hierarchicus* (1966)—with the Brahmins at the top and untouchables at the bottom. He also maintained that castes are linked via a system of ritual acts associated with notions of purity and pollution. Other scholars writing in the period immediately before and after Independence interpreted caste from a more economic perspective, often focusing to a greater extent than Dumont on how caste was actually experienced and lived on the ground, rather than relying heavily on ancient texts for information. These anthropologists showed how at the village level a dominant set of 'patrons', who usually owned the majority of the agricultural land and had the best social/political contacts outside the village, often made payments to a range of clients, usually in kind rather than cash. Patrons were usually from a relatively high jati within the varna hierarchy, but they were not necessarily Brahmins. In this system, the jatis surrounding the dominant caste tended to perform particular hereditary occupations, such as carrying water, washing clothes, or making shoes. There were fairly strict norms in these contexts around the sharing of food and bodily contact, and Dalits were forced to live in specific parts of the village and banned from using higher-caste temples or water sources. Most castes only married within their caste, and there were also other rules, for example that a specific sub-caste could not marry within their own sub-caste or that of their paternal and maternal grandparents, to take the case of the Jats of western Uttar Pradesh. Village ethnographies suggested that low castes had often absorbed the idea of themselves as 'low status'.

While this system of 'unequal interdependence' existed in some form in large parts of India in the middle of the 20th century, a good deal of circumspection is required when generalizing about caste in India. Many of the anthropological studies were conducted with men. There is also a relative lack of information on caste in urban India during the colonial period.

Furthermore, it is not at all clear that, insofar as a strong system of unequal interdependence did operate in 1947, it also did so in earlier periods. One of the important developments in the anthropology of India in the 1960s and 1970s was a shift in view away from the idea that India had a set of distinct cultures—for example of caste—that anthropologists could project backwards in time, towards the appreciation that caste changes in response to shifting economic and political conditions. Within India the sociologist Rammanohar Lohia (1910–67) was especially influential in this respect. In Lohia's view, caste needs to be analysed historically and with respect to how it relates to other forms of inequality—an argument that Minu would keenly understand.

This point is important because there is good evidence that caste hierarchies, as reflected in a system of unequal interdependence, were not a timeless feature of Indian society. Rather, the strength of hierarchical forms of caste and of unequal economic relationships among castes in mid-20th-century India reflected the effect of imperial rule. In particular, the British consolidated and shaped the expression of caste in India. They did so in five ways. First, they incorporated caste into the census. Some pre-British administrators used caste to categorize sections of the population in the subcontinent, but the British did so more assiduously. People were required to list a caste or tribe in a context in which they had multiple, shifting loyalties and identities.

Second, the British attached racial stereotypes to the characteristics of particular castes and used these prejudicial views as a basis for selecting specific jatis to serve for the British. This was evident for example in relation to the army. The British labelled particular castes 'brave and loyal'—such as the Jats—and created regiments for such castes. More notably, the British cultivated higher-caste elites in order to create a cadre of Indians who could assist with the administration of India. It tended to be higher castes that studied in British-inspired educational institutions. This reflected a combination of factors: colonial stereotypes which made it easier for higher castes to enter these institutions, a desire among higher castes to take advantage of colonial channels of advancement, and the greater wealth of many higher castes, which made investment in education possible.

Third, the British used people's jati and position within the varna hierarchy as a type of shorthand for identifying their characteristics and motivations. For example, British colonialists identified some tribal populations—such as the Khangars in Bundelkhand—as threats to civilized society and instituted a Criminal Tribes Act (1871) to manage these populations. According to colonial officials, these tribes were congenitally predisposed to illegality and crime was passed down from father to son. The British chronicled the practices of the alleged criminals, who could be searched and arrested without warrant and had to report weekly to police stations. By 1947, there were 13 million people belonging to 127 communities marked as 'criminal', and they were not freed of this label until 1952. The label of criminality became an important mechanism through which imperialists managed potentially unruly populations in areas of India that were difficult to administer. Reflecting a colonial preference for sedentary populations, it was often the itinerant nature of particular castes or tribes that led them to being labelled 'criminal'. The criminal tribes sometimes fought back against the negative connotations of presumed criminality; but they suffered long-term poverty and stigma.

A fourth point is that the British used caste as a basis for developing a fledgling form of positive discrimination. The British legislated against untouchability from as early as 1858, when a low-caste boy was refused admission into a government school in the town of Dharwar in south India. Throughout the second half of the 19th century, the British discussed the condition of the so-called 'depressed classes', and in 1932 the British proposed that 'untouchables' should be provided with separate electorates in provincial elections. Gandhi went on an indefinite hunger strike in protest at this move, which he thought would drive a wedge between Dalits and the remainder of Hindu society. But he subsequently came to a compromise with Dalit leader Bhimrao Ambedkar: Dalit voters would not constitute separate electorates, but the 'depressed classes' would be granted a greater share of reserved seats within provincial legislatures—an agreement codified in the Poona Pact of 1932.

In the mid-1930s the British then identified a set of castes and tribes that should receive special treatment from the government on the grounds of their having suffered historical disadvantage. Lists were drawn up—called 'Schedules'—of the affected jatis, giving rise to the terms 'Scheduled Castes' (SCs) and 'Scheduled Tribes' (STs) that would qualify for reserved seats in the Government of India Act (1935).

A fifth development, less directly a result of British intervention, was the rise of anti-Brahmin movements in India in the period between 1850 and 1947. This had different strands. In Maharashtra, Jyoti Rao Phule (1826–90) and his wife Savitribai Phule (1831–97) engaged in social reform. They established schools for low-caste children, campaigned for 'untouchable' rights, and challenged Brahmin rituals. In the three decades prior to Independence in Tamil Nadu E. V. Ramasami (1879–1973), popularly known as 'Periyar', who was from a merchant family, was also crucial in mobilizing for Dalits' rights, establishing a Self-Respect League in 1926 that sought to abolish caste and improve women's position in society. Notable low-caste mobilization also occurred prior to Independence in Punjab, where the Adi-dharam movement, led by a Dalit named Mangoo Ram (1886–1980), sought to improve Dalits' position vis-à-vis higher castes. An even more prominent activist was Ambedkar, a Dalit with doctoral degrees from Columbia and the London School of Economics who became a highly successful lawyer and intellectual. Ambedkar wrote of the need to challenge and ultimately eradicate caste, for example in his 1936 book *The Annihilation of Caste.* He campaigned relentlessly around Dalits' rights in Maharashtra and nationally, often creating links between the discussion of India's Independence and the need for low castes to be independent of exploitation and oppression.

None of these anti-Brahmin and low-caste political endeavours owes a direct debt to British rule. But British imperialism and the colonial approach to caste provided the means for Dalit intellectuals such as Phule and Ambedkar to acquire education and express and disseminate their ideas. In addition, colonial policies often had the unwitting effect of spotlighting higher castes' (especially Brahmin) social advantage, thus galvanizing opposition among putatively 'lower' castes.

A sharply hierarchical caste system is therefore not necessarily a natural feature of Indian society. Caste is rather a social institution that has changed historically in response to economic and political forces. The British simultaneously codified caste, as they did religion, but also provided some of the resources and circumstances for change. In so doing, the imperial power introduced or exacerbated social contradictions that continue to mark the lives of low castes in India in the contemporary period, as Minu understands.

Chapter 4
Making India work?
1947–1989

What of hope? The emergence of India as an independent nation was associated with a new institutional drive, centred on the state, to cultivate hope. Independence marks a turning point in the development of what can be termed 'modern' India, for all the evidence of aspects of modernity in the late 19th and early 20th centuries. Yet the post-Independence period also witnessed the successive failure of the state to fulfil people's hopes—to address the problems of poverty and inequality that became so evident during the period of British Rule. Indeed, in some respects successive political regimes have unwittingly exacerbated the scarcities and inequalities that affect Prempal, Hemlata, Minu, and Afrozi.

On the evening of 14 August 1947, Jawaharlal Nehru made a speech to the people of India in which he spoke explicitly of 'hope'. With Independence, he said, 'A new hope comes into being, a vision long cherished materializes.' At this time, plans were already under way for India's 'tryst with destiny', as Nehru put it. The British had initiated the process of drafting an Indian Constitution in March 1946. A Constituent Assembly was charged with producing the document and Nehru (Figure 7) and Ambedkar were key members of the Assembly.

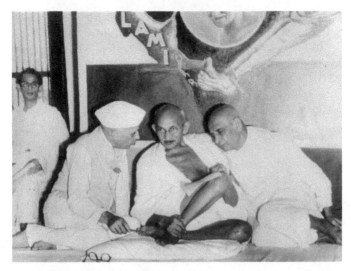

7. **Mahatma Gandhi with Jawaharlal Nehru and Sardar Vallabhbhai Patel, 1946.**

The Constitution, published on 26 November 1949, established
India as a sovereign democratic republic. A President would serve
as formal Head of State and an elected Prime Minster would lead
the executive branch of government. An upper house (Rajya Sabha)
of the new Republic would consist of members appointed by the
President and elected by the states and territories. The lower house
(Lok Sabha) would contain politicians directly elected to represent
constituencies across India in a first-past-the-post system and
for a period of five years. This arrangement bore the imprint of
Westminster-style democracy, and there were other connections
to India's colonial experience. Just as the British had been keen to
prevent the provinces acquiring too much power in their reforms
of 1909, 1919, and 1935, so Nehru and his associates regarded
a centralized system of power as the most effective mode of
government. The centre assumed control over defence, economic

planning, and national security. The states presided over education, health, power, roads, agriculture, and urban development.

Beyond the details of government, however, the Constitution was a statement of intent. It set out how leading thinkers imagined a free India. The spirit of the French Revolution seemed to infuse the document, but more than anything it was a response to British imperialism. In the new India, people were to be citizens, imbued with clear rights. Responsibility for the nation ultimately and inviolably lay with 'the people'. The preamble to the Constitution stated:

> **WE, THE PEOPLE OF INDIA,** having solemnly resolved to constitute India into a **SOVEREIGN DEMOCRATIC REPUBLIC** and to secure all its citizens:
> **JUSTICE,** social, economic and political;
> **LIBERTY** of thought, expression, belief, faith and worship;
> **EQUALITY** of status and of opportunity; and to promote among them all;
> **FRATERNITY** assuring the dignity of the individual and the unity of the Nation;
> IN OUR CONSTITUENT ASSEMBLY this twenty-sixth day of November, 1949, do HEREBY ADOPT, ENACT AND GIVE TO OURSELVES THIS CONSTITUTION

The Constitution identifies a range of 'Fundamental Rights' for India's citizens, including rights to equality, freedom, religious belief, cultural and educational expression, and property. Discrimination along the lines of sex, religion, and caste is established as an offence, and untouchability is outlawed. The Constitution also established equal voting rights for all adults in the country.

At the same time, the Constitution's Directive Principles of State Policy outlined measures to bring about social change (these were not enforceable by a court): Article 39 notes a need to ensure that poor communities receive legal aid; Articles 41–3 enjoin the state to try to secure work, a living wage, and social security for its citizens; and Article 44 indicates that the state should devise a uniform civil code that would replace the personal laws associated with particular religions. Other articles deal with such issues as the need for free and compulsory education, adequate healthcare, and the protection of the environment. The Constitution also contained measures to ensure that quotas within government educational institutions and public-sector employment would be reserved for India's Scheduled Castes and Scheduled Tribes.

The radical nature of the Constitution should be stressed. It was an extraordinarily ambitious legal document. It proposed universal suffrage at a time when Australia did not extend the vote to Aboriginal people. The Constitution reflected on positive discrimination at a point in history when the USA, for example, had not drawn up such measures. The Constitution contains a detailed set of ideas about how a just society should be ordered and how government should pursue development on behalf of the people. It is one of the longest and most comprehensive constitutions in the world.

But a gap became glaringly evident between what was outlined in the Constitution and Indian realities. Ambedkar himself put it eloquently:

> On the 26th of January, we are going to enter into a life of contradictions. In politics we will have equality and in social and economic life we will have inequality. In politics we will be recognizing the principle of one man one vote and one vote one value. In our social and economic life, we shall, by reason of our social and economic structure, continue to deny the principle of one man one value.

In 1950 India—which had a population of roughly 350 million people—was a poor and mainly rural country. Agriculture accounted for 51 per cent of India's national income in 1950–1 and more than 70 per cent of the workforce. The manufacturing sector, by contrast, accounted for just 25 per cent of GDP and 12 per cent of the workforce. The life expectancy in India in 1950 was 40. Only 27 per cent of men and 9 per cent of women could read. Bengal was still recovering from one of the worst famines of the 20th century, and the country bore the scars of its bitter and violent separation from what was then termed East Pakistan and West Pakistan.

India was also highly complex socially and politically—an assortment of territories, including former governor's provinces of British India, princely states, and provinces administered by a chief commissioner appointed by the President. In 1960 the journalist Selig Harrison suggested that India was on the verge of falling apart: 'The odds are almost wholly against the survival of freedom...The issue is whether any Indian state can survive at all.' Ambedkar himself warned that, if the contradictions between political and socio-economic rights were not addressed in the new India, 'Those who suffer from inequality will blow up the structure of political democracy.'

India survived in part because increasing sectors of society came to feel involved in the political process, especially via the ballot box, minimally during a first period of broadly effective leadership under Nehru, more meaningfully in the more competitive political environment associated with Prime Ministers Indira Gandhi and her son Rajiv Gandhi, and even more so during a more open period of democratic participation characterized by the rise of low-caste political parties and Hindu nationalism after 1989. It was not simply a matter of 'hope springing eternal' but of a democratic system providing the institutional mechanisms for sections of society to feel at least a measure of involvement in government and perceive grounds for optimism.

Nehru (1947–1964)

Nehru's rise to power in the post-Independence period might appear at first blush to be a natural process given his stature in the

Congress Party. In fact, it owed something to chance. Mahatma Gandhi had stepped back from leading the new nation. Then, in 1948, Nathuram Godse, a member of the Hindu far Right, assassinated Gandhi outside Birla House in New Delhi. About two years later, Nehru's main rival for power in the Congress, Vallabhbhai Patel, also died.

Five factors ensured India's survival and growth in the decade and a half that Nehru was at the helm. The first was strong leadership. Nehru was widely admired. He had charisma and a formidable intellect. Nor was Nehru a new leader thrust into the limelight. He had been a stalwart of the nationalist movement. Nehru was particularly skilled in managing regional powerholders and politicians, and careful not to accede to ad hoc demands, for example for the creation of new states within the Indian federation. If Nehru felt threatened, he was not afraid to act. He made use of British preventive detention laws to lock up many of the Communist leaders who opposed him, for example. Congress also orchestrated central government takeovers of state governments that did not conform to the central government's agenda, for example in Kerala in 1959.

Second, Nehru was able to develop an economic plan that gave some stability to the Indian economy and provided a basis for future development. He regarded himself as a socialist, not in the sense of advocating the national ownership of property and land but in wanting the state to be the guarantor of economic and social rights. Influenced also by the modernization theories of the time, especially the writing of the economist Arthur Lewis, Nehru specified a need to move India from agriculture to manufacturing. The Second Five-Year Plan (1956–61), produced under the direction of P. C. Mahalanobis, fleshed out this vision of economic transformation. The government would use indirect taxation—from sales tax and excise tax, for example—as well as foreign aid and money borrowed from the Reserve Bank of India to boost key areas that had been critically neglected by the British during imperial rule, especially the production of steel, power, and chemicals. Nehru imagined that these industries would in a second phase fuel the development of Indian-run manufacturing companies producing items such as bicycles and radios for the Indian consumer.

Nehru's economic policies did not generate additional employment. Moreover, because his attention was on investing in industry, agriculture tended to suffer. The annual growth in the productivity of agriculture in the 1950s and early 1960s was only around 3 per cent. Nehru made no attempt to introduce a robust system of taxation in India and this undermined the revenue base for investment in public infrastructure or welfare. Nothing like a national education or health system emerged in India in the period after Independence.

Nor did Nehru have the will or capacity to reform landownership in a meaningful way. South Korea's remarkable economic growth in the third quarter of the 20th century owed much to its strategy of breaking up large estates and creating a productive agricultural sector based on small, owner-occupied plots. Nehru was aware of the need for such reform and promoted various 'land to the tiller' initiatives. But opponents in Congress prevented Nehru from engaging in wholesale reorganization, and local elites were often able to prevent the effective implementation of laws.

Yet the rate of economic growth of India during the 1950s and 1960s was good relative to the first fifty years of the century under colonialism and satisfactory when judged against the experience of other 'developing countries' during the period. Nehru's investments in manufacturing helped to diversify the economy and the emphasis of the Five-Year Plans on building industry across India's regions spread economic development into areas that might otherwise have been marginalized. In addition, Nehru's capacity to begin to industrialize the country—industrial growth rates were at roughly 7 per cent per year over the 1950s and 1960s—provided some of the infrastructure required for subsequent economic expansion.

The third aspect of Nehru's strength as a leader, and of the strength of the Congress Party, lay in his capacity to develop a fairly robust democratic system of rule that staved off serious political unrest. He presided over the creation or consolidation of democratic institutions that underpinned India's effective functioning. This included the emergence of the Supreme Court as a final arbiter on legal issues, the Indian Administrative Services (from the colonial Indian Civil Services), the Planning Commission charged with formulating economic policy, and the Electoral Commission, responsible for the safe and efficient conduct of elections. Nehru was able to guarantee India's emergence as a secular democratic polity in part through preventing the military threatening executive power. Pakistan, by contrast, suffered a military uprising in 1958 and subsequent coups in 1977 and 1999.

Nehru also ensured that the Congress Party was pre-eminent politically, lending stability to his economic and foreign policy projects. The British first-past-the-post electoral system ensured that Congress commanded large majorities in parliament, despite not winning a majority of the votes in any elections in the twenty years after Independence. Congress success also partly reflected the party's capacity to absorb and encompass multiple viewpoints during the 1950s and early 1960s. In addition, it reflected its tight organization. The Congress was in truth comprised of a federation of units that insulated it from effective challenge. At the regional and local levels, party bosses—also termed 'big men' or 'brokers' (*dalaal*)—disbursed jobs, money, or political help in exchange for support during elections. This system, which built upon a pre-existing patronage economy propagated by the British, ensured some ideological acceptance among the poor.

Nehru was also effective in accommodating political pressures. There were calls within India for using the principle of language to carve up India's constituent states. This found expression in a report by the States Reorganization Committee in 1955, which recommended that common language should be the chief principle for delineating states. A subsequent 1956 Act cemented this move. While Nehru had feared the political consequences of the reorganization, it had the opposite effect to some degree of welding the new nation together.

Not all of Nehru's success in the political realm can be attributed to the man himself; his opponents were in relative disarray and the general social condition of the people discouraged organized critique. At the relatively everyday level, the caste system divided people and also served to legitimize the authority of the higher castes in power. Literacy rates were low, newspaper penetration was limited, and there was minimal access to radios until transistors proliferated in the mid-1960s. Moreover, the political Right made relatively little headway during Nehru's tenure in power. S. P. Mookerji, a former President of the Hindu Mahasabha, established the right-wing Hindu nationalist Jana Sangh in 1951, which contested the 1952 general elections. It had powerful ideological roots in Savarkar's Hindu nationalism and the RSS. But the Jana Sangh could not command the type of popular support or organizational capacity of the Congress in the 1950s and 1960s and thus remained on the margins of electoral politics.

A fourth main dimension of Nehru's power was his view that religion and caste should not shape politics. Nehru was an atheist. He believed that the importance of religion, and with it caste, would gradually recede in independent India. Reflecting this view, Nehru had little enthusiasm for using religion or caste as bases for positive discrimination in independent India. Nehru's approach to caste inequality was to use economic and social programmes to raise people out of poverty. He had to moderate this view throughout his period as a leader in India and in the face of demands from low castes for reservations. But Nehru's approach discouraged aggressive caste-based or religious-based political assertion.

Fifth, Nehru managed to avoid major sustained conflict within India or between India and other nations. His assumption of power coincided with the beginning of the Cold War between the USA and Soviet Union. Nehru ensured that India remained non-aligned—neither associated too closely with the USA nor with the USSR. This allowed India to make a series of strategic deals with both the Western and Eastern blocs, exploiting its position as a neutral state to obtain resources for human development and technical assistance.

Nehru faced stiff challenges in the diplomatic and foreign policy sphere, however. In October 1950 China annexed Tibet. Nehru did not feel he could risk a war with China over this act and in 1954 India recognized Tibet as part of China. Nehru also visited China that year. At the same time, Nehru remained privately suspicious of the Chinese government. Any warming of relations between the two countries ended in 1959, when Nehru gave sanctuary to the 14th Dalai Lama, and then more markedly in October 1962 when China and India began a war over the boundary between Indian and Chinese territory in the Himalayas. The war ended with a Chinese declared ceasefire in November 1962, which led to a consolidation of borders along what the Chinese called the 'Line of Actual Control'. Nehru more than doubled the size of the Indian army in the two years following the ceasefire.

India's relations with Pakistan were even more fraught. This partly related to the issue of the division of water resources between Pakistan and India. The relationship between the two countries also hinged on the crucial question of Kashmir. The region of Jammu and Kashmir was not part of either India or Pakistan at Independence. After partition, Pakistan controlled the western part of the Princely State of Kashmir and the northern territories of Gilgit-Baltistan. However, the Kashmir Valley, Jammu, and Ladakh—what became

'Jammu and Kashmir'—was established as a state within the Indian federation, the only state with a majority Muslim population.

Jammu and Kashmir's national belonging was a difficult issue. It was ruled by a Hindu Maharaja, but had a majority Muslim population. Popular sentiments within Kashmir were divided between those who wanted to join Pakistan, those who aspired to be part of India, and those wanting an independent state of Jammu and Kashmir. At the time of Independence, Jammu and Kashmir were amongst a handful of princely states that did not decide to accede to either India or Pakistan. In October of 1947, however, a group of armed tribal Pathans from Pakistan invaded Kashmir to 'liberate' its Muslim population. The Maharaja, supported by the popular Jammu and Kashmir National Conference, signed an agreement to accede to India on the condition that the Indian army fight off the invasion. This precipitated the first India–Pakistan War, which lasted until 1948. The war was inconclusive, leading to contested borders between the two countries, which remain a burning issue today.

Jammu and Kashmir was incorporated into India under Article 370 of the Constitution. The article granted the state a somewhat different status relative to others. Among the most important provisions of the article was the stipulation that the centre could only legislate in relation to Kashmir with respect to defence, foreign affairs, and communications and that the Constitution of India need not be wholly applicable to Kashmir. During the 1950s Nehru contended with a range of different factions within Kashmir that periodically called for the state's independence. Although Nehru had promised Chief Minister Sheik Abdullah a plebiscite on the issue of Kashmir's independence, he later reneged. He considered control over Jammu and Kashmir crucial to the integrity of the Indian nation and of symbolic value—having a Muslim majority state within India gave weight to his claim that India was a secular nation, marginalizing the perspectives of his Hindu nationalist rivals within Congress.

Indira Gandhi and Rajiv Gandhi (1964–1989)

Nehru died in 1964. Around this time, his industry-led economic approach was beginning to unravel. A series of agricultural failures had led to rising prices and depressed internal consumer demand. India faced a mounting balance of payments crisis that saw it become reliant on foreign aid. Lal Bahadur Shastri (1904–66) replaced Nehru as Prime Minister in 1964 and was responsible for managing these economic dangers. In 1965, the World Bank reported that India needed to give a greater role in the economy to private capital and also place greater emphasis on agriculture. The US government responded by making any further grants of food aid to India contingent on a change of economic approach. Political problems compounded the gathering economic crisis. Pakistan's attempts to establish an insurgency inside Jammu and Kashmir led to the expensive Indo-Pakistan War of 1965, a war that also further encouraged the USA and other countries friendly towards Pakistan to withdraw foreign aid.

In the face of these pressures and drought in India, but also reflecting an ideological change within government, a new Agriculture Minister, 'Chiddy' Subramaniam, shifted the emphasis of economic planning somewhat away from industry and towards agriculture. He emphasized technological change in farming and a role for High Yielding Varieties of wheat and rice. The resulting 'Green Revolution' entailed farmers placing greater emphasis on the use of chemical inputs to agriculture with positive effects on yields. At the same time the Food Corporation of India was established to purchase grain at fixed prices from farmers, which could then serve to prevent famine and malnutrition via a public distribution system wherein food would be disbursed at subsidized prices. The Green Revolution was also associated with a drive to electrification. Electricity had previously been largely limited to metropolitan India but the government sought to extend it throughout rural India from the mid-1960s onwards, in particular.

Any immediate turnaround in India's fortunes seemed unlikely. Lal Bahadur Shastri died in January 1966 and senior Congress leaders installed Indira Gandhi, Nehru's daughter, as Prime Minister. The combination of economic difficulties at home and rising military spending meant India lacked money to import food. It therefore took the decision to avail itself of a US 'Food for Peace' programme—authorized by Public Law 480 (PL-480)—which allowed poor nations to pay the USA in their own currency for food. Under US pressure, Indira Gandhi also devalued the rupee in 1966 and liberalized its import policy. The public bitterly resented the move, which contributed to rising food prices, and was seen as a sell out to the USA. In 1967 general elections opposition parties attacked Congress rule with a new vigour. After the elections, the Congress majority in the Lok Sabha was reduced to twenty-five.

The Congress system, whereby regional and local Congress representatives provided jobs or government largesse for political support, was breaking down, and so too was the close communication between the Congress Party at the state level and the Congress Party at the centre. Indira formalized this division by taking the decision to delink national and state elections in 1971. At the same time, Indian politics was becoming more competitive. The Communist Party of India had split in 1964, leading to the formation of a splinter party, the CPI (Marxist), more sympathetic to China and radicalism. Shortly afterwards, the so-called 'Naxalite movement' began in 1967 in the village of Naxalbari in West Bengal when communist students and peasants started an armed struggle demanding the abolition of landlordism. It subsequently became the inspiration for the Communist Party of India (Marxist-Leninist) and its attempts to initiate a rural-led revolution to overthrow the state.

In 1969 the Congress Party also split. On the one hand, a Congress (R), including Indira Gandhi, rhetorically at least supported a socialist approach. On the other, Congress (O) was associated with a relatively reactionary set of politicians, including Morarji Desai.

The 1966 devaluation and partial liberalization inaugurated a period of low economic growth that was to last through to the mid-1980s. Economists typically explain this low growth with reference to a shopping list of economic mistakes: the state's inability to raise income tax; a failure to raise domestic demand due to a focus on large-scale heavy industry; and the failure to reform agriculture to give land to those actually cultivating. Indira Gandhi enacted policies in the period beteen 1969 and 1973 that tightened state control over the economy and complicated any effort by private business to promote growth, such as the nationalization of the banks and introduction of legislation that regulated big business. Yet Indira's economic strategy in 1966 worked in some respects. She prevented famine—by 1970 India was self-sufficient in food—and brought the fiscal deficit under control.

In the meantime, in the political sphere, Indira had to contend with a major shift in the nature of politics that cannot be understood solely as a function of her own actions. At the time in India, there was a general political awakening associated with steadily rising literacy rates, people's greater exposure to news via transistors, and growing assertion from a wide variety of groups expressing regional, caste, or sectoral interests. It was a time of flux wherein politics itself was becoming increasingly democratized. In the words of two famous political scientists, India was moving in the late 1960s from a phase of 'command politics' under Nehru to 'demand politics' under Indira and her successors. A scarcity of everything—educational opportunities, jobs, development resources, political seats—encouraged a whirl of political bargaining, no longer closely controlled by the Congress but manifest still in the activity of numberless patrons and brokers across India.

Indira (Figure 8) reacted to this fevered political environment by stressing her own direct connection to the poor. She employed populist phrases such as '*garibi hatao*' (abolish poverty) aimed at deepening her connection with the masses. In the early 1970s this strategy seemed to work. She inaugurated rural development programmes aimed at marginal farmers, labourers, and the poor, and including schemes aimed at employment generation, poverty alleviation, and various forms of social support. The scale, depth, and intensity of poverty in India at the time was such that these programmes would only ever be 'the cumin seed in the camel's mouth', to use a popular Indian phrase, but they made a difference to some people and they bolstered Indira Gandhi's reputation. She routed her opponents in the March 1971 elections. In the same year she successfully provided military support for the Bangladeshi nationalist movement in a thirteen-day war with Pakistan that led to the establishment of Bangladesh as a separate nation.

At the same time, however, Indira Gandhi concentrated power on herself and was capable of authoritarian measures to defend her position. In 1975 the Allahabad High Court ruled that Indira Gandhi had been guilty of electoral malpractice in the 1971 elections. She also faced a pressing threat from a student movement led by the Gandhian activist J. P. Narayan in central India, which was opposing corruption and demanding a 'total revolution' in Indian society. Indira Gandhi asked the President to impose a State of Emergency. She argued that protests were undermining the government and economy and issued a twenty-point plan to get the economy back on track. But detractors pointed to the Emergency as evidence of Indira's predisposition to anti-democratic, heavy-handed tactics. During the twenty-one-month Emergency, Indira quashed organized criticism, locked up political adversaries, and banned student groups. Curbs were placed on the press and Indira used the national broadcaster Doordarshan for spreading propaganda. The Emergency was associated with the abuse of political power, including slum clearances and a forced sterilization drive orchestrated by Indira's son Sanjay Gandhi. When Indira Gandhi

8. India's Prime Minister Indira Gandhi speaking to supporters in
June 1975.

eventually called elections in March 1977, a disenchanted electorate voted her out.

The success of the oppositional Janata Party in the 1977 elections, led by Morarji Desai, marked the first time that the Congress had not presided over Independent India. The Janata Party offered a platform to relatively prosperous farmers, who had benefited from the Green Revolution and had considerable political influence in rural areas. These farmers began to argue that Indian government policy had been unfairly skewed towards urban areas, the so-called 'urban bias' argument. The rich farmer Charan Singh, a leader of the farming lobby and Finance Minister for a brief period in 1979, was especially instrumental in seeking to extend new opportunities and resources to farmers (a contemporary of Singh's joked that his budget 'smelled of the soil'). Agricultural subsidies increased and the government moved to raise the prices it offered farmers for key agricultural goods. Farmers' movements emerged in India, such as the Bharatiya Kisan Union in north India led by Mahendra Singh Tikait, and the Shetkari Sanghatana led by Sharad Joshi in the west. Their populist rhetoric was notable at the time for its insistence on identifying a traditional, rural, farmer-centred India—a 'Bharat', a Hindi term for India—that could be counterposed to the modernizing drive of urban 'India'.

There was also a consensus within the Janata Party around the need to decentralize power. This was reflected in the emphasis that the party placed on appropriate technology, a fashionable term at the time in development theory, and a move to strengthen local government 'panchayats', a term for a local council, which was the basic unit of government across India.

Factionalism quickly weakened the Janata Party, however. In 1980, the Congress Party returned to power under Indira Gandhi, who as in an earlier period focused power on herself and her immediate coterie. From 1980, Indira Gandhi sought to develop a more pro-business approach to the economy, for example by reducing corporate taxes. This change of tack encouraged faster economic growth. At the same time, however, much of the Prime Minister's attention was occupied with dissent within India. The shift from command politics to demand politics continued apace. The regional party Dravida Munnetra Karagham (DMK), which emerged in Tamil Nadu in 1949, was increasingly assertive. It aimed to represent the interests of Dravidians at both state and federal levels and opposed the imposition of Hindi as the national language. In addition, the Communist Party of India (Marxist) (CPI-M) consolidated its position in West Bengal in the early 1980s. Moreover, the Telugu Desam Party, under the leadership of N. T. Rama Rao, rose to power in Andhra Pradesh, toppling Congress in 1983. The TDP claimed to represent the Telugu people and consolidated a support base among moderately wealthy castes.

In north-west India greater tension was evident. The Akali Dal sought to establish a separate Sikh nation in Punjab. Indira Gandhi tried to seed divisions in the Akali Dal through supporting the intervention of an orthodox religious leader, Jarnail Singh Bhindranwale, in the politics of the region. When Bhindranwale himself turned hostile to Congress, however, Indira adopted a violent approach, storming the Golden Temple in Amritsar, a supremely holy site for Sikhs, where armed militant followers of Bhindranwale were hiding. In revenge for this act, two of Indira's Sikh bodyguards assassinated the Prime Minister in her home in Delhi on 31 October 1984. This incident sparked an anti-Sikh pogrom in Delhi, which claimed several thousand lives.

Indira Gandhi's son Rajiv Gandhi rose to power in a wave of sympathy for the death of his mother and committed himself to continuing the legacy of his family. Rajiv promised to continue a programme of rural development and build on India's strategy of non-alignment with regard to major powers.

Rajiv Gandhi also pledged to root out corruption. Bribery was hardly new. But in a context of intense competition for political office since the late 1960s, politicians spent increasingly large sums of money seeking to be elected. Furthermore, the delinking of central and state elections meant that competitions for seats were occurring more frequently. After achieving success, politicians needed to recoup their money and did so through extracting funds from senior government bureaucrats who in turn took illegally acquired money from their inferiors. The result was a vast type of 'trickle up' system entrenched within bureaucracies such as the police and rural development offices. Rajiv once noted that of every 100 rupees intended for the poor in the villages, only Rs 17 ended up in their hands. As India had become more genuinely democratic in terms of a plural set of voices capable of bidding for a share of the spoils, so it became increasingly difficult to govern. It was at roughly this time that Salman Rushdie famously quipped, 'Indian democracy: one man one bribe.'

Rajiv is less well known for his anti-corruption efforts—in fact he actually became embroiled in corruption scandals in the late 1980s—than he is for his embryonic efforts at economic reform. He used the 1985 budget to make India more business friendly. Rajiv Gandhi reduced corporation and personal income taxes with a view to promoting private sector growth, deregulated the cement industry, and introduced a greater degree of competition into several key sectors of the economy. GDP growth rates averaged nearly 6 per cent per year over the 1980s.

In 1987 Congress suffered electoral losses in Haryana in the midst of significant corruption scandals, and in the late 1980s Rajiv retreated often to the type of heavy-handed approach that had been characteristic of Indira Gandhi when she had felt most threatened. There were several issues that Rajiv mishandled, including elections in Kashmir, which were rigged by the central government. A Tamil extremist assassinated Rajiv Gandhi in 1991 in protest against the Prime Minister's management of Tamil politics in south India and Sri Lanka.

'Demand politics' took yet another twist with the rise of V. P. Singh, a politician who traded on his reputation as 'Mr Clean'. In October 1987 Singh had launched the Jan Morcha (people's platform), and he won a victory in a Lok Sabha by-election in Allahabad in 1988. In August of the same year V. P. Singh developed a National Front of seven parties lined up against Congress and including the Janata Party, Lok Dal, and Jan Morcha, which formed later that year into the Janata Dal. In the 1989 elections the Janata Dal were outperformed by Congress but still managed to form a minority government with outside support from the Hindu nationalist Bharatiya Janata Party (BJP). A 'National Front' government was born that managed India until 1991 and witnessed the development of crucially important new trends.

Chapter 5
Rethinking India

The period between 1989 and 1992—roughly the period during which the National Front government presided over India—was pivotal in the development of the country. Three key shifts were especially important each of which, as Stuart Corbridge and John Harriss have pointed out, was associated to a certain extent with a 'reimagining' of India as a country and of the ideas that underpinned Nehru's period of rule. The first major change relates to caste. Caste reservations became a major political issue in the late 1980s and early 1990s and low castes became much more powerful within politics. The political commentator Yogendra Yadav referred to this trend as a 'second democratic upsurge'—the rise of regional and farming lobbies in the mid-1960s being the first.

In the Poona Pact of 1932, Congress pledged a certain number of seats to be reserved for 'depressed classes' (Dalits) in provincial legislatures. In 1942, following input from Ambedkar, the colonial government allowed 8.5 per cent reservations for Scheduled Castes (SCs) in central government services. The need for reservations in education and public services was indicated in Article 46 of the Constitution—but attempts to implement these were challenged in various courts. In response to this, and despite a lack of support from Nehru, an amendment to the Indian Constitution in 1951 clarified that nothing in the Constitution would 'prevent the state from making any special provision for the advancement of any socially and educationally backward classes of citizens or for the scheduled castes and scheduled tribes'. Thereafter, the central government and state governments institutionalized reservations for SCs and Scheduled Tribes (STs) in education and the administration. These were supposed to be temporary measures.

In the meantime, in the 1950s, Nehru had established a commission to examine the case for extending reservations to so-called 'Other Backward Classes' (OBCs)—also called 'Backward Castes'—castes that were 'above' SCs and STs in Hindu caste hierarchies but nevertheless suffered from social or economic discrimination and disadvantage. The commission reported the existence of several thousand jatis who might legitimately make a claim to be 'backward' and recommended that they receive compensatory discrimination. But Nehru regarded implementing this recommendation as too politically hazardous. In the late 1970s the Janata Party set up a second government commission to investigate the issue, which was under the chairmanship of B. P. Mandal. The 'Mandal Commission' reported in 1980, again identifying several thousand jatis as potential recipients of reservations. Again, the central government ignored the recommendation. But in 1989 V. P. Singh did act on the Second Commission. He promised that the government would introduce a 27 per cent national-level quota for OBCs in educational institutions and public-sector enterprises. This came on top of an existing 22.5 per cent combined quota for SCs and STs, bringing the total reserved quota to 49.5 per cent. Upper castes—especially students—reacted furiously. Some estimate that over 150 students attempted to burn themselves alive in protest against OBC reservations in 1989 and 1990. At the same time, some jatis that had historically been trying to claim a high place within the varna hierarchy began to change tack and stress instead their lowly standing in order to qualify for OBC reservations.

One corollary of the rise of the OBC reservations issue was the growing strength of OBC regional and national leaders. Figures such as Laloo Prasad Yadav in Bihar and Mulayam Singh Yadav in Uttar Pradesh could exploit the strong feelings of OBCs in defence of compensatory discrimination. They also built a sense of backward caste pride, often invoking symbols of their jati background and claiming a more direct connection with people on the ground than that established by mainly upper-caste politicians in the past. There were strong elements of an Indira Gandhi-type populism to such strategies, but in some respects OBC politicians did break the mould, talking pragmatically about the need to address the core concerns of OBCs around education, jobs, and access to state assistance, for example. The anthropologist Lucia Michelutti has described this process as the 'vernacularization' of democracy.

During the late 1980s and early 1990s, Dalits also became much more active in politics, reflecting in part the emergence of a cadre of low-caste leaders who had benefited from reservations. This Dalit upsurge took different forms across the country. In Madhya Pradesh a higher-caste-dominated Congress Party sought to partner with Dalits to raise their standing, with limited success in terms of improving the lot of SCs. In Tamil Nadu, an explicitly Dalit party tried to capitalize on grassroots mobilization to become a major state player, again with rather limited results. In Uttar Pradesh (UP), low-caste politics was slightly more successful in effecting ground-level change. A Dalit named Kanshi Ram founded the Bahujan Samaj Party (BSP) in 1984. Drawing on the support of the state's large Dalit population, the BSP formed coalition governments in UP in 1993, 1995, 1997, and 2002, and then won power on its own in 2007. Mayawati, a Dalit woman and ex-schoolteacher, has led the BSP since 1995. Under Mayawati, the BSP tried to improve Dalits' access to development resources such as education, enhance their representation in local government and bureaucracies, and transform the iconic landscape of the state through the construction of symbols of Dalit pride. Ironically, given Ambedkar's insistence in his lifetime that he should not be made into an icon, Ambedkar statues across India now outnumber those of any other political leader. They usually depict a man wearing a suit, carrying a briefcase, and with a pen in his top pocket—an image that conveys professionalism and service. So symbolically loaded have Ambedkar statues become that in the 2012 elections in Uttar Pradesh, they were covered with blankets to prevent the images sparking discord. Low castes across India now organize Ambedkar birthday celebrations and processions and use statues as a focal point for play readings, recitations, and other events.

The efforts of political parties such as the BSP to improve Dalits' standing and confidence interacted with changes in the nature of the local government. In 1992, the 73rd Amendment Act was enacted to increase the power of local government. It implemented a three-tier system in which local panchayat councils would play a central role in the provision of public services and implementation of development programmes. The Act also stipulated that panchayat elections should be held every five years and provided a periodic 33 per cent reservation of panchayat seats for women, STs, and SCs. In some cases, this institutional shift has improved Dalits' power at the local level.

A second shift in the nature of Indian politics that is especially associated with the early 1990s relates to the rise of Hindu nationalism. The Bharatiya Jana Sangh, also known as Jan Sangh, had merged with other parties to form the Janata Party in 1977. In 1980 it reformed itself as the Bharatiya Janata Party (BJP) and continued in its goal of prosecuting a Hindu nationalist agenda. The BJP first contested elections in 1984, when it secured 8 per cent of the vote in the Lok Sabha. Their vote share rose to 20 per cent in 1991 and 26 per cent in 1998, when Atal Vajpayee of the BJP was able to form a government as part of a National Democratic Alliance (NDA). Between 2004 and 2014 a Congress government held power in India under Manmohan Singh. In 2014, however, support for the BJP surged to 31 per cent in the Lok Sabha election. Though not commanding a majority of the popular vote, India's first-past-the-post system delivered the BJP a substantial majority in the Lok Sabha. This was the first majority government in India since 1984. Since 2014 Narendra Modi, the charismatic BJP politician, has led India (Figure 9).

Prime Minister Modi links the two key political shifts of the early 1990s together. He is from a Backward Caste and made considerable play of his humble background and OBC status during the run up to elections in 2014. Modi is also a representative of the Hindu Right, with a reputation for pushing forward Hindu nationalist ideologies while Chief Minister in Gujarat.

Drawing on the Hindu nationalist ideas of figures such as Savarkar and Gowalkar, the BJP during the 1990s, 2000s, and 2010s has periodically stressed the fundamental 'Hindu roots' of India. This came to be labelled 'Hindutva' philosophy—the idea that it is India's manifest destiny to be Hindu, that all living in the territory of India are 'culturally Hindu', and that it is the duty of the government and prominent people in society to espouse the benefits of Hinduism. In this vision, Hinduism is imagined as a

9. Prime Minister Narendra Modi of India during an Oval Office visit to United States President Barack Obama at the White House, Washington DC, 30 September 2014.

religion that encompasses others. Many Hindu nationalists picked up Savarkar's claim that Buddhism and Jainism, being indigenous to India, were simply atheistic (*nastika*) branches of Hinduism rather than separate religions.

The early 1990s, in particular, also witnessed a flourishing of a more menacing set of arguments that depicted Muslims and Christians as somehow un-Indian and which exploited religious communal tensions. This cultural drive was led by the RSS and the Vishwa Hindu Parishad (VHP), which was formed by senior RSS leaders in 1964 with the intention of uniting and organizing those whom it had identified as belonging to a broad 'Hindu' tradition, including Jains, Buddhists, and Sikhs. RSS and VHP leaders have been outspoken in claiming their intention to protect Hinduism from what they see as aggression from other 'groups'—particularly Islam, Christianity, and secularism.

In many situations, the BJP during the period between 1989 and 2016 acted as a check on extremist tendencies within the RSS and VHP. Under Prime Minister Vajpayee, for example, the BJP resisted calls by the RSS and VHP to repeal Article 370 that gave a special status to the state of Kashmir. Vajpayee's reputation as a unifier carried over to foreign policy. He initiated a new peace process aimed at resolving the Kashmir dispute. The Lahore Declaration (1999) emphasized dialogue, mutual trade, and friendship.

At other moments the BJP seemed to line up with the RSS and VHP in assertive 'campaigns'. For example, liberals criticized the Vajpayee government for not doing more to prevent Hindu–Muslim violence in Gujarat in 2002. At a more mundane level, Vajpayee presided over an administration that undermined secular education through the rewriting of history textbooks to reflect a glorified Hindu past—part of what some have termed the 'saffronization' of education (saffron being a holy colour for Hindus). In addition, the BJP under Vajpayee conducted nuclear tests in May 1998.

For many on the Hindu Right, the testing was of a 'Hindu bomb', with extremists calling for a militaristic Hindutva drive.

Another aggressive move on the part of the Hindu Right—and a lightning rod for religious communal violence—was a campaign in the early 1990s to tear down the Babri Masjid, a mosque in the city of Ayodhya, Uttar Pradesh. In spite of the absence of archaeological evidence supporting the case, RSS volunteers argued that Muslim invaders had destroyed a Hindu temple to the deity Ram in order to build the Babri Masjid. In 1984 the VHP demanded that the mosque be demolished. On 5 December 1992, while a BJP government was in power in Uttar Pradesh, the VHP stage-managed the destruction of the mosque. The demolition triggered riots in various parts of urban India, including Bombay.

Under Modi's prime ministership, the Hindu Right has again been emboldened on the national stage. Although his tenure as Prime Minister has not led to major religious communal riots, it has raised tensions in a number of areas. This includes the issue of the coercive reconversion of non-Hindus 'back' to Hinduism, furore over the protection and veneration of cows, and continued concerns over the role of the Hindu Right in sponsoring cultural and educational drives aimed at instilling intolerance. This assertiveness has also been associated with a crackdown on dissent that, while stopping well short of Indira's assertiveness during the Emergency, has resulted in the increased monitoring of universities, researchers, NGOs, and individuals whose views contradict those of the ruling Hindu elite. In this respect Modi's leadership partly reverses the general trend towards democratization that is a feature of the period between 1989 and 2016. The broad point remains, however: if Nehru's rule can be imagined as a period of elite-dominated politics, and the 1967–89 period is posited as one of continued Congress dominance but with incursions from OBCs and others, the post-1990 period is an age of truer democratization.

Economic reform and rising prominence

A third major shift occurring in the early 1990s was economic reform. This had begun under Indira Gandhi and Rajiv Gandhi, but India's economic crisis in the early years of the 1990s triggered more substantial 'liberalization'. During the 1980s, foreign and domestic government borrowing was responsible for fuelling much of the economic growth. In 1991 the Indian government, facing a balance of payments crisis, introduced reforms of the economy that were aimed at enhancing the role of the private sector in the economy, encouraging foreign direct investment, and freeing capitalists from unhelpful government regulation. The first major wave of these reforms was pushed through under the prime ministership of Narasimha Rao, who headed a Congress-led coalition government in India between 1991 and 1996, and his lieutenant Dr Manmohan Singh, who served as Finance Minister under Rao before becoming Prime Minister himself.

Reflecting Nehru's interest in developing a planned state economy, the government during the first four decades of Indian Independence had exerted a strong hand over the process of industrialization. Entrepreneurs wishing to start a new business had to apply to many government agencies for permissions (licences). The state could also largely direct companies with regard to what they made, how much of a product was made, and how it was sold. This complex system became known as the 'licence raj' or 'rule by licences'. In the early 1990s the government moved to abolish licensing in all but a handful of industries.

Economic reforms also included new measures to encourage foreign direct investment in India, which grew from $US132 million in 1991–2 to $US5.3 billion in 1995–6. In addition, the Indian government partially removed tariff and non-tariff barriers to economic trade and abolished import licensing. The economic reforms resulted in a major boost for the Indian economy, which grew at between 5 and 7 per cent per year from the mid-1990s to 2002 and then at about 9 per cent annually between 2003 and 2008. Services accounted for the majority of this growth, especially construction, business services, and insurance—reflecting the rise of internal (India-based) demand.

Since his inauguration as Prime Minister in May 2014, Modi has sought to extend the reforms. He has tried to deregulate the pricing of natural gas and kerosene, remove government support prices for agricultural goods, reform bankruptcy laws, and increase foreign investment in insurance, defence, construction, retail, coal mining, and e-commerce, among a number of sectors. This work is ongoing, with the exception of the bankruptcy laws, which have passed. Modi has also attempted to develop a new means of disbursing money from the state to the poor via direct benefit transfers into people's bank accounts. In addition, Modi has pushed forward the goal of introducing a Goods and Services Tax (GST) that would replace a plethora of ad hoc taxes and serve as a comprehensive indirect tax on the manufacture, sale, and consumption of goods and services in India. The Lok Sabha passed the GST Bill in August 2016.

Economic growth in India has interacted with the expansion of India's diaspora population to deliver benefits to the Indian state. There are estimated to be between 25 and 30 million people of Indian origin living around the world, with especially large populations in the USA, Saudi Arabia, the United Arab Emirates, Malaysia, and the United Kingdom. In the USA, the number of migrants from India soared in the 1990s, such that they now represent one of the largest migrant communities—second only to migrants from Mexico. Though the Indian diaspora is highly diverse in terms of socio-economic background, in the USA many Indians occupy senior positions, particularly in management, business, services, and sciences. On average, they have considerably higher incomes and levels of employment than other migrant communities, and with more than 76 per cent of Indian-born Americans holding a bachelor degree or higher, they are almost three times more educated than people born in the USA.

The Modi government has harnessed the power of the Indian diaspora. India received an estimated 70 billion US dollars in global remittances in 2014, more than eleven times the contributions made in the mid-1990s. The current government has also built upon the expertise of the diaspora: in Modi's words, to turn the 'brain drain' into a 'brain gain'. For example, Modi's social media strategy draws in large measure on the expertise of the Indian diaspora. The government is facilitating investment through its Indian Diaspora Investment Initiative and is encouraging youth of Indian origin to undertake internships in India. The Indian government is also attempting to lever the diaspora as a diplomatic tool, particularly in the USA.

Modi has been unapologetic about his lack of interest in the Nehruvian Non-Aligned Movement and has attempted to position India as a key ally of the United States. This may reflect a belief that such an alliance will counterbalance the economic ascendancy and increased assertiveness of China within Asia. At a more regional level, India under Modi also appears to be giving up old commitments. Modi has shown considerably less enthusiasm for the South Asian Association for Regional Cooperation and is looking instead to South-East Asia and partners in the Indian Ocean for cooperation on both security and economic development.

A further sign of India's changing position in the world, supported by economic reform and growth, is its relationship to aid. In 2015, the UK ceased to provide India with official development assistance, citing India's many millionaires and space programme as signs that India no longer needed their support. Many other developed countries followed suit. A number of Indian politicians welcomed the move, seeing it as unbefitting for a rising superpower to be an aid recipient. Indeed, India is increasingly a provider of aid. Since the mid-1990s, its aid contributions have risen sharply, with a particularly dramatic rise since 2010. In the 2015–16 budget, India allocated $US1.6 billion in aid, mostly in the form of bilateral assistance.

Like most 'developed' countries, India's aid contributions are not driven purely by altruism. In 2015–16, 84 per cent of India's aid was directed towards neighbouring south Asian countries, reflecting its interest in ensuring stability in the region and consolidating its status as the regional hegemonic power. There are also economic motivations: 63 per cent of India's 2015–16 aid contributions went to Bhutan, mostly to develop hydroelectric power, which is in turn exported to India at cheap rates. But India has slowly expanded the geographic reach of its aid, with a rising proportion being allocated to countries in Africa and South-East Asia. This reflects the growing importance of so-called 'South-South Development Cooperation'. As a post-colonial country with first-hand experience of the challenges of development and receiving foreign aid, India is advantageously positioned to mobilize its expertise to assist other developing nations.

Poverty and inequality

Economic reforms reduced 'poverty' quite markedly. According to the World Bank, the proportion of Indians earning less than $1.90 per day fell from 45.9 per cent in 1993 to 21.2 per cent in 2011. But India's economic growth has not been as effective at reducing poverty as economists and others might have expected. Indeed, the 'poverty efficiency' of India's growth—its efficacy as a tool of poverty decline—was only roughly half that of China's through the 1990s and 2000s.

This is partly because economic reform has occurred in the context of marked social inequalities and has widened those inequalities. In 1991, the richest 1 per cent in India controlled 37 per cent of the national wealth. In 2016 they controlled 58 per cent of the wealth.

10. Dharavi slum, Mumbai, 2007.

India is more unequal on this measure than any other major economy in the world, excepting Russia (Figure 10).

On the other hand, a middle class has grown up rapidly since 1990 as a direct result of economic reforms and accompanying economic growth, although it is still somewhat smaller than many India boosters will admit. The Centre for Global Development found that there were 69 million Indians (roughly 6 per cent of the total population) earning between $US10 and $US50 per day in 2010, which they take as a measure of middle-class status. This 'middle India' has some knowledge of English, is mainly but not exclusively urban, and has often embraced new opportunities to acquire consumer goods and, to a lesser extent, to obtain access to new earning opportunities, for example in the IT sector, real estate, and finance. Their power relative to the lower middle class and poor also resides in their range of social contacts, education, and capacity to communicate advantage via their speech, clothing, homes, and possessions. The Indian middle class is now widely identified outside India as a key market for global corporations. Within India, commentators frequently depict this class as the

79

brash, self-confident representatives of a globally assertive 'new India'.

Social inequalities reinforce and exacerbate economic ones. India remains a deeply patriarchal country and in many respects economic reforms have deepened gender divides. Far fewer girls are enrolled in school than boys. Men are massively over-represented in politics, high-paid jobs, and influential positions within civil society. Moreover, gender violence is rife. The period of economic reform coincided with an increase in reports of domestic violence and violent action linked to the prevailing system of arranged marriage, especially dowry, which is associated with the harassment of young brides. The shocking rape of a young woman on a bus in Delhi in December 2012 put these issues at the forefront of national and international consciousness. Aside from a thin upper stratum of people in metropolitan areas, women continue to struggle to convince senior family members of the value of women obtaining paid work outside the home and of their right to participate in civil society and politics.

It is therefore unsurprising that women remain well behind men in every indicator of social development in India, as they do in many other parts of the global South. Perhaps most notably, the sex ratio in India declined from 972 women to every 1,000 men in 1991 to 933 in 2011. This disparity in the size of the male and female population cannot be put down to migration. Rather, it reflects the practice of sex selective abortion, made possible by the availability of new ultrasound technology, and to the preferential care that many parents devote to sons with treatable illnesses such as diarrhoea.

At the same time, caste difference and caste-based inequality has received a new lease of life, not only through reservations and the rise of low-caste political groups that use caste as a rallying call but also as a result of caste-selective processes of recruitment into

modern jobs. Elite business enterprises in India as well as
prestigious schools and universities have frequently found subtle
ways to exclude those from lower-caste groups. The survival
of caste as a marker of distinction is also evident in terms of
the prevailing arranged marriage system, where jati is often
a primary consideration when arranging a match. Low castes
remain behind high castes on most development indices and
in most areas of India. Discrimination against Dalits associated
with the stigma of 'untouchability' has become less common
but remains prevalent. Dalits are frequently not permitted to
enter temples and suffer other forms of routine exclusion
and discrimination.

Religion is another major axis of difference and inequality.
The particular disadvantage of Muslims in modern India—who
numbered 138 million in the 2011 census—was strikingly revealed
in the government of India's Sachar Report published in 2006. This
report showed that Muslims lag behind Hindus, and even Dalits,
in terms of education. Between 1983 and 2000, the percentage
of Muslims completing primary school rose by 15 per cent, but
the equivalent figure for Dalits was 19 per cent. Even allowing for
Muslims' low education, they suffer from disadvantage in terms of
labour market access. Muslims also often face particular difficulties
acquiring healthcare. None of these forms of disadvantage can be
pinned directly to the effects of economic reform. The point rather is
that liberalization, while reducing poverty, has not fundamentally
altered the life chances of many within the Indian population.

The economic reforms also exacerbated inequalities between the
urban and the rural. The reforms reduced the availability of cheap
institutional credit in the countryside. In several states there was
a slowdown in the growth of the agricultural area under irrigation,
use of electric power, and cropping productivity in the years
following the reforms. Even where liberalization did not undermine
agriculture directly, it often heightened farmers' fears regarding
access to government subsidized, favourable prices for their

products, electricity supply, and state protections from foreign competition. In many regions of India it is women who are left to tend rural plots—often no larger than kitchen gardens in the context of land subdivision—while men migrate in search of work. The prevalence of farmer suicides in India in the 21st century also bears testament to these sectoral inequalities.

Economic reforms also deepened regional divides. Rich states in the south and west have fared much better than poor states in the north and east. This is partly because states that are already successful in terms of infrastructure and countering corruption are better able to attract foreign investment. It also reflects the manner in which reforms have reduced possibilities for the central state to redistribute resources from relatively wealthy parts of India to other regions. There have been various efforts to identify a cluster of especially precariously positioned states—Uttar Pradesh and Bihar are always among them—where development indicators are extremely low.

People are being removed from poverty in formal terms, but at the same time actually feel that they are poorer. This is the case in part because of a human tendency to measure one's progress relative to others. If a few people in a region are becoming very rich, one's own meagre gains feel like losses. Champions of economic reform are wont to argue back that if growth improves everyone's lives somewhat it does not matter if the rich are becoming much richer. But inequality has net social and political costs that cannot be assuaged by pointing to the economic gains provided to the poorest in society.

Even aside from these arguments about whether absolute poverty reduction should be lauded even as perceived relative poverty deepens, official definitions of poverty obscure the hardships of India's poorer households. People may be earning more but able to buy less in terms of a large and diversified food basket. Over the past few years key components of the poor's diet, for example lentils and vegetables, have become more expensive in many parts of India thus undermining the nutrition of the poor. More generally, people—while becoming slightly richer—are often excluded from acquiring health, education, and sanitation. Economic reforms led to a relative decline in government spending on education, healthcare, urban infrastructure, and power transmission.

The persistence of poverty and inequality, in spite of democratization and economic reform, puts the question of hope under the spotlight. Why has hope survived? Why has there not been a large-scale popular uprising in India? Part of the answer lies in the capacity of successive governments—Nehru, Indira, and Modi, for example—to deliver some gains to the poor and to provide new narratives of hope.

Chapter 6
Social revolution

Any discussion of sources of hope in modern India must take account not only of the progressive democratization in formal, party politics associated with the rise of non-Brahmin political parties and politicians since the mid-1960s (and especially since the 1990s). It must also consider a social revolution. This has provided people, elites in particular but also some other sections of society, with new economic and social aspirations communicated via phones, the internet, and schooling.

India's social revolution has three main aspects. First, there has been a transformation in people's access to communication technologies. The number of people with a mobile phone subscription rose from 2 million in 2000 to 980 million in 2015 in India. Some caveats are in order. Only a fifth of Indians had direct access to internet technology in 2014, well below the figure in other BRICS countries. Moreover, according to one report, women in India are 27 per cent less likely to have access to the internet than men. Yet the expansion of mobile phone ownership and internet technology is remarkable, reshaping possibilities for participation in civic life. As Robin Jeffrey and Assa Doron have shown in their book *The Great Indian Phone Book*, the poor benefit a great deal from having access to a mobile phone. They do so in part through the everyday access that their phones provide to friends, colleagues, hospitals, and local government agencies.

Mobile phones have also been important in political organizing associated with the rise of low-caste parties in India.

Less tangibly, but equally importantly, the rise of new communication technologies has helped to fuel aspirations. It has encouraged people to reflect on the manner in which individuals in more prosperous parts of India and the world conduct their lives.

What is also remarkable about the mobile phone revolution in India is the extent to which technology has been used as a basis for development initiatives. For example, the NGO Sahayog based in Uttar Pradesh has inspired women to use their mobile phones to document the illegal charges that government health workers demand for public services. As another example, the Sesame Workshop India has used mobile phones and other digital devices to bring their Muppet programme *Galli Galli Sim Sim* to remote locations and have developed educational resources linked to the show.

The state has also used the communications revolution to develop new schemes. As part of its Digital India initiative, the Modi government has established more than 250,000 Common Services Centres throughout the country. These centres allow citizens to access government services, print identification cards, register to vote, and acquire passport services. They also serve as a portal for adult education and digital literacy courses and for access to services from the private sector, from mobile phone recharges to bank loans.

A second aspect of the social revolution relates to education. There is enormous enthusiasm among parents and young people for education in contemporary India. Across a wide variety of areas and among people of almost all economic and religious backgrounds, citizens argue that formal education has an intrinsic importance—it is a social good 'in and of itself'—and has an instrumental value: it provides people with the capacity to act confidently in society, participate in politics, acquire employment, and be afforded respect. Education, more than any other development, has greatly increased people's propensity to hope and talk about 'hope', either in relation to themselves or their children.

School enrolment has increased sharply. The number enrolled in secondary school grew from about 50 per cent in 2004 to 75 per cent in 2014. Similarly, the proportion of those attending college or university in the relevant age group jumped from 6 per cent in 1983 to 18 per cent in 2014. The literacy rate in India rose from 52 per cent of the population in 1991 to 74 per cent in 2011 (Figure 11).

The educational revolution is in turn linked to a third key shift related to notions of citizenship and the state. There was a time when political scientists stressed the alien nature of notions such as 'citizenship' in India. India, we were told, operated according to other laws. Caste, religious community, and family provided people with their moral compass rather than abstract and imposed ideas of the bureaucratic state. Associated with this argument was the notion that somehow it is inappropriate to bemoan corruption in India because the term is not understood in India in the same way in which it is used in the West.

Such arguments may have made sense as recently as the 1980s. But it is now very difficult to find someone in India willing to defend corruption in the sense of the abuse of public office for private gain. There has been a marked increase in the extent to which people have come to absorb, respect, and fight for the norms of liberal government: democratic representation, an impartial bureaucracy, and a fair legal system. People have encountered these liberal democratic norms in school, university, via the media, and through their exposure to local and international NGO and government pronouncements.

11. Children studying on tablets in Varanasi, Uttar Pradesh, 2015.

Cultural expression

Social revolution has encouraged cultural expression. The most obvious example is Bollywood. In the 1970s in the West 'Bollywood' was a diminutive and somewhat patronizing term for Indian cinema. By the 2000s, however, Bollywood had become a major player in the global entertainment industry. The granting of industry status to film making and increased corporate involvement in Bollywood since the early 2000s has led to a massive injection of capital. The proliferation of multiplex cinemas has also boosted profits. In 2012, Bollywood produced four times as many films as Hollywood and sold more than twice as many tickets. Reflecting this growing global appeal, the International Indian Film Academy Awards is held in a different country each year and Hollywood actors are frequently appearing and even playing major roles in Hindi films. To take just one example, in the 2010 film *Teen Patti*, Ben Kingsley played alongside Amitabh Bachchan.

Relatively mainstream Bollywood films are tackling challenging social issues, often in ways that reflect more liberal, cosmopolitan sensibilities than Hindi films of the past: *3 Idiots* (2009) explored flaws in India's education system; *PK* (2014) was a satirical take on religion and religious divisions in the country; *Pink* (2016) drew attention to problems relating to sexual violence against women.

There is also growing scope for actors to move between Bollywood and other types of cinema and small-scale film industries and cross-cultural collaborations are being initiated in regions outside the Mumbai stronghold. There are also other regional traditions of film springing up such as Mollywood (Malayalam cinema), Jollywood (Jharkhand cinema), Pollywood (Punjabi Cinema), and—most significant after Bollywood in terms of revenue—'Kollywood', named after the Kodambakkam neighbourhood of Chennai in Tamil Nadu.

Beyond film, there are a plethora of forms of cultural expression that owe much to India's recent social revolution. For example, in parts of West Bengal, rural intellectuals have revitalized popular theatre to engage with issues as diverse as marriage, identity, power, and rural livelihood. Street theatre organizations in Delhi have been similarly influential in contesting some of the changes that have been made in the city related to planning, slum clearance, and road development.

The number of documentaries made on India has also grown enormously. Many of these are controversial and most reflect the growing confidence of India's activist citizens. Noteworthy examples of influential documentaries include *Katiyabaaz* (2014), which documents Kanpur's electricity crisis, frequent load shedding, and the theft of electricity by entrepreneurs. The Uttar Pradesh Chief Minister reportedly requested engineers at the Power Department to watch the film so that they could devise solutions to stop illegal connections. Similarly, activists are making use of video and the internet to reach global audiences. A good recent example is 'Kodaikanal Won't', Sophia Ashraf's adaptation of the Nicki Minaj song 'Anaconda', which draws attention to the mercury contamination of Kodaikanal after a leak from a Unilever factory.

At the same time as new technological opportunities have emerged, Indian citizens have done much to protect traditional forms of cultural expression. In the literary field, the recent global success and influence of Indians is remarkable. Since the mid-1990s, India has had three Booker Prize winners: Arundhati Roy for *The God of Small Things* in 1997, Kirin Desai for *The Inheritance of Loss* in 2006, and Arvind Adiga for *White Tiger* in 2008. Indian writers have also courted global controversy including Salman Rushdie, whose work *The Satanic Verses* led Iran's supreme leader Ayatollah Khomeini to order a death sentence against him for alleged blasphemy.

Another example of the continued importance and growth of traditional forms of cultural expression is the 'ghazal' (religious song). There is now a huge trade in CDs of popular ghazals, including thriving regional markets for devotional and secular songs. The scholar Peter Manuel has done more than perhaps anyone else to chart how technological change has revitalized this and other music traditions. Manuel shows that the introduction of cassettes in the 1980s in India decentralized regional music production and circulation. The increased use of mp3 formats in the early 2000s reinforced this process. Informal regional music markets are able to produce a constant flow of new DVDs—including ghazals—often in sync with local religious celebrations.

Religion has also boomed in India in the wake of increased education, the rise of citizenship ideals, and improvements in communication technology. Often there has been a shift towards more personalized forms of religion as exemplified in the figure of Sathya Sai Baba (1926–2011), who claimed to be a reincarnation of Shirdi Sai Baba, a saint from Maharashtra who died in 1918. He attracted an enormous following and his Sathya Sai Organization, which funded various spiritual education centres, was worth Rs 400 billion at the time of his death. His teachings have been regarded as significant in the current era of globalization, as they strip Hinduism of its more esoteric trappings and its myriad regional and caste-based variations. Instead of appealing to a particular local community, they putatively address 'humanity' as a whole. Similar interpretations have been made of organizations such as the Brahma Kumaris World Spiritual Organization, Sri Sri Ravi Shankar's Art of Living Foundation, and the yoga guru Baba Ramdev, who all teach Indian spiritual traditions in ways that do not require strict adherence to particular communal identities.

Traditions of pilgrimage and religious expression have also prospered in many areas as people, more educated and better able to communicate across space, re-engage with this stock of knowledge and practice. The government website for the *Kumbh Mela*, a major Hindu pilgrimage, claims that 120 million attended the 2013 festival in Allahabad, up from 40 million in 2001 (Figure 12). In addition, donations to local temples form a large part of the philanthropic contributions of the rich within India and of the Indian diaspora, motivated by religious or caste solidarity or, in some cases, as a way of acquiring prestige. For example, the Swaminarayan community has gone from being a localized religious sect from Gujarat to a nationally recognized organization through the construction of its lavish Akshardam Temple in Delhi in 2005.

India's social revolution, far from consigning regional and religious 'traditions' to the sidelines, as Nehru might have imagined when embarking on his post-Independence modernization drive, has lent new power and reach to such dynamics. They have also provided opportunities for Hindus in particular to brand and market the type of approach to life emphasized by Vivekananda over 100 years ago, giving new support for the project of developing a global 'Hinduism'. As Vivekananda suggested on his visit to the USA, and as is more palpably evident today, cultural globalization is a multi-centred process emanating not only from Western centres such as New York and London but also from Mumbai, Delhi, and Kolkata as well as second-order cities such as Patna, Meerut, and Pune.

Civil society

A related effect of the social revolution has been to boost very significantly the importance and activity of civil society in India. A civic upsurge has occurred in tandem with the waves of democratization identified in Chapter 5, especially the 'second wave of democratization' of the 1990s and 2000s.

Civil society in India has not been strong historically, in large part because the British prevented dissent. There was a public arena

12. Holy men and devotees bathing at the Kumbh Mela, Nasik, Maharashtra, India, 30 November 2015.

associated with the middle classes in 19th-century India, most obviously expressed via religious reform movements and the nationalist movement. The agitations of the 1930s and 1940s for self-rule widened the base of this civic action. But the rise of mass civil society is recent in India, reflecting a change in Indian citizens' understanding of themselves in relation to the state and the world.

The new civil society can be traced in part through reference to the rise of relatively large-scale visible social movements. The Right to Food Campaign is a notable example. This national-level coalition works to ensure that all people are free from hunger and malnutrition. It does so by promoting livelihood security and ethical food systems. The Right to Education Movement has been equally important in campaigning for increased public funding of state education and opposing the privatization of schooling. Perhaps even more important still, a vibrant Right to Work movement played a crucial role in the formulation of the National Rural Employment Guarantee Act (2005) and has since campaigned for the scheme's successful implementation.

The Anna Hazare anti-corruption movement is another noteworthy example of the expression of people's desire for change in their relationship with the state. The Gandhian activist and rural development worker Anna Hazare came to prominence in 2011, when he held a hunger strike in Jantar Mantar, New Delhi, on the issue of corruption (Figure 13). The act captured the public's imagination, in part as a result of the charisma of Hazare, but also because 'corruption' is an issue that connects together a myriad of frustrations that citizens experience in their interactions with the state, for example in relation to education, acquiring development resources, and seeking healthcare.

Hazare demanded the formation of a Jan Lokpal in India. This would be an institution that would monitor and investigate political corruption and impose punishments on officials guilty

13. New Delhi, India, 23 February 2015. Veteran Gandhian Anna Hazare addresses farmers during his protest against the ordinance on the Land Acquisition Act.

of graft. Hazare's hunger strike drew support from people throughout the country and inspired further campaigns by other activists, including Baba Ramdev, who led a movement for the repatriation of black money held abroad. Arvind Kejriwal's involvement as an organizer of Hazare's 2011 movement was, in many ways, the launching point for his political career as leader of the Aam Aadmi Party.

The explosion of civil society associated with India's social revolution is also evident in an upsurge in NGOs in India. Economic reforms increased the access of NGOs in India to foreign funds and boosted the overall number of organizations. India currently has an estimated 3.1 million NGOs. Some focus on social action. For example, the Barefoot College in Tilonia, Rajasthan, established by the activist and intellectual Bunker Roy, provides education for both adults and children, particularly those who dropped out of formal education. The college also addresses the basic needs of locals, ensuring access to clean water, housing, and health services.

Another notable example of NGO strength in the social arena, and of the power of charismatic individuals to transform India, is the work of Nandan Nilekani and Rohini Nilekani in the sphere of philanthropy and education. The couple initiated the EkStep Foundation in the 2010s, which aims to bolster Indian students' literacy and numeracy skills through digital media. The foundation is developing easy-to-use apps that are constantly improved through the collection of data on student progress.

There are numerous less heralded but equally impressive forms of social action occurring within the NGO sphere in India, such as the work of Sonali Nag. As Associate Director of the Promise Foundation, Nag contributed towards developing educational interventions in India that draw on the latest scientific evidence from the psychology of learning. The Foundation has developed targeted interventions for children with learning difficulties and those at risk of dropping out from school.

Some NGOs in the social sphere employ irony to prosecute their goals. For example, an NGO called Fifth Pillar has been prominent in the anti-corruption field through its use of a 'Zero Rupee note' to promote social change. Fifth Pillar produced the note as a means of embarrassing officials who request bribes. When faced with a request for a service that is officially free, a citizen of India, armed with the note, can present zero rupees. The note carries a picture of Gandhi with the message 'I promise neither to give nor receive a bribe.' There are 2 million of the notes now in circulation in India, and Fifth Pillar claim that their endeavour has had a marked effect on corruption in some spheres.

The vibrancy of India's civil society is also manifest in the frequency with which people link issues of rights to aspects of identity and cultural practice. The Humsafar Trust, founded by

Ashok Row Kavi in the late 1980s in Mumbai, for example, provides services and advocacy for LGBT citizens of India. The Trust's projects focus on health and support services for gay and transgender people. They also facilitate friendship groups and a sense of community amongst LGBT youth.

The environment is another key area for emerging NGOs. Environmental consciousness was galvanized in India by the Bhopal Disaster in 1984, in which a gas leak from a pesticide factory resulted in thousands of deaths. In the years since, NGOs have been at the forefront of fighting for justice for victims. But it is climate change that has been the most important spur to NGO action in the environmental sphere. India is particularly vulnerable to climate change. Diminishing rainfall, increasing frequency of droughts, and a more erratic monsoon threaten agriculture, and sea level rise would pose a major risk to low-lying cities such as Kolkata and Mumbai. Reflecting the work of NGO pressure groups, India was an early mover in raising awareness about the projected impacts of climate change and is beginning to make important efforts in the sphere of climate change mitigation—solar energy capacity doubled in India in 2016.

Some commentators such as the public intellectual Partha Chatterjee have objected that Indian civil society remains dominated by elites. There are obviously instances where well-meaning people 'at the top'—or among the middle classes—fail to address the more pressing needs of those on the ground or claim to speak on behalf of 'the India poor' in ways that reflect their own quest for aggrandizement. Many among the poor feel removed from possibilities for meaningful participation in civil society, in part because of other demands on their time and in part because the gains of such action are not always apparent.

Yet one of the notable features of several recent civic and NGO initiatives has been the manner in which the wealthy and relatively poor have worked together to foster innovative change.

A notable example here is the variety of self-help groups that have emerged in poorer areas of major cities, which often swap ideas for urban small-scale development with other units in other parts of India and other parts of the world, supported but not directed by the urban upper middle classes.

This point also emerges strongly when we consider how civil society is intertwined with the state. In the judicial arena, for example, state-sponsored tribunals work in tandem with local people to address areas of concern. Governments form tribunals to arbitrate within specific domains—either to increase the efficiency of the judicial system or to facilitate input from those with specialist knowledge. They range in scope from the Central Administrative Tribunal, which deals with disputes between public servants and the government of India, to the Film Certification Appellate Tribunal, which hears appeals regarding the issuance of film classification and certification.

Again, the environment is a prominent focus for organizations in this field, and the National Green Tribunal (NGT), which was established in 2010, has engaged in especially pioneering work in the area of environmental protection and natural resources. In one prominent case managed by the tribunal, cyber café owner Ramesh Agarwal lodged an appeal within the NGT against the granting of environmental clearance for Jindal Steel and Power Ltd for the construction of a large coalmine in Raigarh, Chattisgarh. The NGT found that the corporation had failed to hold adequate public hearings regarding the environmental impact of the mine despite concerns of its impact on the local population and hence cancelled environmental clearance. In another major verdict, the NGT cancelled environmental clearance for a hydro-power project in Arunachal Pradesh, in response to a case lodged by a group of Buddhist lamas. It was found that the project would have a serious impact on the wintering site of the black-necked crane, a bird held to be sacred by the local Buddhist population.

Another wellspring of civic innovation involving elites and the relatively marginalized working together is the Election Commission. The Election Commission of India has been a dynamic institution, evolving to changing circumstances and making use of innovations to ensure fair elections and overcome the potential for corrupt interference. In the 2007 Uttar Pradesh elections it used its newly digitized electoral rolls to map villages that had not voted during several previous elections. The Commission is thereby able to identify sections of society who had been pressured into not voting. Moreover, between 2009 and 2014, the Commission implemented a series of innovations to ensure greater voter awareness and participation, which they termed SVEEP—Systemic Voters Education and Electoral Participation—and included the use of social media and 'voters' festivals' to encourage higher voter turn-out.

Rethinking civil society

In his classic work on civil society, the German philosopher Hegel defined the concept as an arena of association, typically formalized within organizations, where people meet as equal citizens to discuss and act upon society. They do so as impartial citizens rather than as members of any particular identity group.

But in India, and reflecting also the effects of British imperialism, civil society often operates through religion and caste rather than on the basis of 'impartial identities'. One example is the RSS, which has seen a very rapid increase in membership since the 1980s, reflecting a wider revival in Hindu nationalism. It has also changed in its form and activities, as its members become more educated and better versed in the norms of government and techniques of effective communication. When it initially formed, the RSS was a paramilitary organization intended to instil militarism and cohesion into Hindu society. At least in the first decades of its existence, the RSS's ideology was focused on the idea of a Hindu nation. More recently, the RSS has emphasized broader social activity, such as the provision of services to the poor. Furthermore, RSS membership has surged and also extended beyond its traditional membership base of Brahmins and Banias to low castes.

Many Muslims in India have formed organizations that operate as elements of civil society. They provide alms to the poor, run schools, and deliberate on matters of public concern. They also provide institutional credit and basic healthcare. Caste can also offer a basis for civil society organizations. There are upper-caste associations, established under the name of a particular caste, that engage in social projects on behalf of poorer members of their caste. In specific regions—although not yet on a national basis—Dalits have also used a common sense of caste identity to establish libraries, schools, rotating credit associations, and other social and economic organizations, as especially evident in the case of the BSP.

In another twist on Hegel's definition of civil society, India's emerging civic sphere is often most evident outside rather than within formal institutions. For example, there has been a remarkable increase in people's use of the Right to Information Act to bring the state to account. The Right to Information Act (2005) granted citizens the legal right to request information from any government body and receive a reply within thirty days. Within just two and a half years, more than 2 million requests for information were lodged and campaigners fought relentlessly to ensure the legislation was properly implemented. Throughout rural India, people have used the RTI legislation to demand information on entitlements to services which they have not received and used that information to identify corrupt officials. Civil society and multilateral development organizations sometimes structure these efforts. The United Nations Development Programme has set up 'RTI Clinics' in rural and tribal areas in Orissa, for example. The Consortium of Groups for Combating against Corruption, a civil society organization working in rural Rajasthan, has facilitated people's use of RTI claims to expose corruption in service provision and prevent further malpractice. But much RTI activism occurs outside institutional contexts through the actions of ordinary citizens.

Constraints

Three significant weaknesses in India's political institutional infrastructure limit civil society and the social production of hope, with particularly negative implications for the poor. The first relates to the law. India has, on the face of it, a well-developed legal system with a strong Supreme Court in Delhi, high courts, and an extensive network of local courts. But India's federal judicial system currently has a backlog of over 20 million cases. There are thousands of prisoners awaiting trial. Corruption, the bribing of advocates and judges, and non-professionalism is rife within the judicial system, especially at the local and regional levels.

Some defenders of India's legal system respond by pointing to the relative professionalism of the Supreme Court. But while the Supreme Court has kept a check on criminalized and corrupt state bureaucracies and reversed some idiosyncratic decisions arrived at lower down, it has done so at the cost of blurring the division of powers on which healthy democracies depend. Functions that should, under the terms of the Constitution, be undertaken by the government or government-appointed bodies are sometimes overseen by the Supreme Court, for example in relation to the closing down of industries that are said to be 'polluting'. The increased use of Public Interest Legislation encourages this arrogation of powers because, under this system, members of the public who have not been directly affected by an action may nevertheless complain about it—to the Supreme Court—and in the process bring the topic at hand under the purview of that Court.

It is also relevant to note that some of the most repressive laws introduced by the British remain on the books. For example, in

2007 the West Bengal government justified the shooting of farmers
who were protesting about the forced acquisition of land for a
Special Economic Zone in Nandigram by citing a 1943 police
regulation that made it compulsory for the police to secure
'immediate effect' by shooting at people and not in the air. Colonial
sedition laws have also been invoked by the Indian state in recent
years as a way of trying to justify the gagging of artists and
intellectuals critical of the government.

A second major check on the effective functioning of civil society
in India relates to the police. Successive post-colonial government
regimes have lacked the political will or know-how to reform the
police in India, which has become a 'service' riven with corruption
and favouritism. The proper duty of the police—to uphold the law
and protect citizens—is derogated in favour of a focus on protecting
the rich. The police in India are often inept, politicized, and
focused on acquiring illegal incomes from their posts. This does not
reflect any deficiency in the quality of recruits but rather the manner
in which everyday discrimination and rampant profit-seeking is
institutionalized within the force. Constables, who make up the
overwhelming majority of police officers, often have to bribe to
obtain their posts and are compelled to pay senior officers regular
sums of money. They are effectively forced in this context to
collect bribes from the public.

Some sections of the police are also rumoured to carry out
extra-judicial killings in India—often euphemistically termed
'encounters'—at the behest of politicians or regional elites.
Moreover, the Justice Verma Committee Report on the police in
India, published in 2013, identified systemic police harassment
of women.

A final check on the proper functioning of civil society in India
concerns the media. India's media is lively, but powerful
institutions have often colonized and co-opted key organs of the
fourth estate. Political parties make large donations to regional

newspapers to ensure favourable coverage. Regional television stations are often in thrall to politicians. Corporations also wield an unhealthy influence over the media due to the reliance of many newspapers and television channels on advertising revenue.

Poverty and inequality in India persist not only because government policies and capitalist development have failed to provide the economic means for mass advancement but also because large sections of the population are not able to participate in civil society in ways that would meaningfully enhance their prospects. This is true in spite of a social revolution that has enhanced people's hopes and provided some possibilities for social action and cultural expression.

Chapter 7
Youth

Through the 1990s and 2000s, Satish Kumar, a student in the north Indian city of Meerut, spent his time seeking an officer-level job in the Indian army. He prepared himself assiduously. But he failed six times. His friends jokingly 'promoted' Satish on every occasion, and he had become Lieutenant-Colonel Satish Kumar by 2005. Satish looked around for other work for a few years and then reconciled himself to being 'unemployed' (*berozgaar*). Eventually, in 2011, he capitalized on the one skill he felt he had acquired in a fifteen-year search for work. He set up a small institute that trained people to prepare for officer-level entry into the army.

One in ten people in the world are an Indian youth aged under 30. This enormous population is poised to make a major contribution to the future of their country. In India as in many countries the hopes of the nation are projected onto youth. But are the conditions in India conducive to young people fulfilling societal hopes? Insofar as they are not—and Satish's story is being played out in many parts of India—what can young people do to improve the situation in which they live?

These questions become more urgent when we consider the structure of India's population. There is a particular concentration in many parts of India of people aged between 20 and 40 that reflects the nature of India's demographic transition. High fertility rates were characteristic of India in the late 20th century. But in the current century fertility rates have started to decline in some areas. This leaves a bulge in the population pyramid akin to the 'baby boomer' generation in the West.

Economists have argued that a large young adult population can be a 'demographic dividend' for a country. A substantial young adult population relative to the number of old people and children is likely to boost a country's savings and reduce the state's spending on welfare. Some of the economic success of east Asian countries in the late 20th century can be attributed to the 'dividend effect'. Yet economists also warn that a country will only benefit from the demographic dividend if the institutional and infrastructural environment is right. Education and healthcare systems should be robust, and corruption should be kept in check. If such conditions are not met, the apparent advantage of a large youth population may turn into a threat—a demographic disaster.

Education

India currently does not provide a context for the demographic dividend effect to occur. The growth in enrolment in education, while important in terms of raising esteem and providing access to basic numeracy and literacy, masks a crisis in effective provision. Outside of a small number of expensive and highly competitive institutions, most schools have inadequate infrastructure and suffer from a lack of curricular reform. Researchers recently found that 25 per cent of teachers were absent from classes during spot checks across India and only 50 per cent of the teachers who were present were actually teaching. The Indian state has consistently failed to raise its spending on education, which remains at roughly 3.7 per cent of GDP, well below the expenditure in many Western countries. Poor educational quality also reflects governance problems. Some states of India, such as Tamil Nadu, Kerala, and Himachal Pradesh, contain relatively well-functioning schools. But in other parts of the country, teachers work in a corrupt system in which it is possible to give bribes for favourable postings or to avoid censure when failing to teach. Forced to study in poor-quality institutions, neglected by teachers, and bewildered by curricula that bear little relationship to their everyday lives, it is hardly surprising that many young people drop out of school, especially girls and those from marginalized communities.

Higher education is also in a parlous state. There were few institutions in India in the top 400 in the QS World University Rankings in 2016 and none in the top 100. India arguably does not contain a single world-class university that encompasses all disciplines. Government spending on higher education remains at only about 0.5 per cent of GDP. Within most colleges and universities the curricula are outdated, there is little continuous assessment or careers advice, and research productivity is low. University lecturers and professors often skip classes in favour of giving tutorials to students outside class for additional fees. Enrolment in private colleges in India grew at 20 per cent annually between 1983 and 2013, but many of these colleges lack trained faculty and pedagogical review. The government's Twelfth Five-Year Plan of 2012 established a National Higher Education Council which offered states increased funding, especially for higher educational infrastructure. But reform is likely to be slow.

In both school and university education the colonial impact on India is still apparent. In many cases, teachers and lecturers responded to the colonial imposition of alien curricula in India by resorting to rote memorization, which came to replace older, richer traditions of learning and instruction. In some cases colonial curricula survive. Even where syllabi have changed, the focus on learning narrowly for examinations persists. Moreover, the general crisis in school and university education reflects the wider point that the British neglected the development of a broad-based educational system in India in the 19th and early 20th centuries.

Vocational education in contemporary India is also in crisis, again partly reflecting both the collapse of manufacturing industry in India in the 19th and early 20th centuries and colonial neglect of industrial training. The litany of problems is long: only 10 per cent of the working-age population in India has any technical training; India currently skills just 7 million people annually; the Industrial Training Institutes that provide vocational skills to students are under-resourced and lack up-to-date syllabi; and roughly 60 per cent of Indian vocational trainers lack professional teaching qualifications. In addition, students are not able to enrol in skills-related courses in school until Class 11 and the vocational system in India is largely delinked from industry. Prime Minister Modi announced a Skill India programme in 2015 to provide vocational training to 400 million Indian workers by 2022 and his government has developed a policy framework for expanding skill training efforts and a separate Ministry of Skill Development and Entrepreneurship. But the impact of such initiatives is often disappointing. In 2015–16, one report suggests that only 80,000 of the 1.7 million youth who participated in the Prime Minister's flagship skills project, the Pradhan Mantri Kaushal Vikas Yojana, obtained work.

These problems with education do not invalidate the argument that the acquisition of qualifications and basic literacy and numeracy skills has been important in the mobility strategies of the poor—a key element of the social revolution. But the substandard state of education prevents non-elites in India from capitalizing on schooling and university learning in the manner that might be predicted.

Health

India has improved healthcare substantially since the 1970s, for
example through the Expanded Programme of Immunization
(1978), which reduced children's deaths from major communicable
diseases. Since the 1970s, there has been a considerable expansion
of healthcare facilities, especially in south India. The infant mortality
rate in India declined from 202 per thousand live births in 1970 to
64 in 2009. Yet the Indian government has failed to increase
healthcare spending beyond 2 per cent of GDP. Primary Health
Centres are often poorly provisioned and neglected. According to
one study in 2002–3 absenteeism rates among health workers
ranged from 35 per cent to 58 per cent across India. As late as
2005, 60 per cent of India's children were malnourished and only
44 per cent fully immunized. Dengue fever, hepatitis, tuberculosis,
malaria, and pneumonia remain deadly and virulent ailments in
India. Moreover, sanitation is poor, increasing the chance of disease:
122 million households in India have no lavatories. Over 50 per cent
of the population defecates in the open. And only 26 per cent of
India's slum population has access to safe drinking water.

A meagre 5 per cent of the Indian population has health insurance,
and according to one estimate 40 million people every year
move into poverty in India as a result of out of pocket expenses
associated with healthcare. Obtaining effective care entails
navigating a landscape in which fraud, unnecessary surgery, and
misdiagnosis are common. This reflects the poor training of many
private doctors, patients' low knowledge base, malpractice by
many unscrupulous agents, and the absence of effective regulation
of private health provisioning. This situation again reflects the
colonial inheritance. The British did very little indeed to build a
public system of healthcare in India. In 1934 there was one hospital
bed for every 3,810 members of the Indian population—less
than one-twelfth of the provision in the Soviet Union at that
time (Figure 14).

14. New Delhi, India. An All India Institute of Medical Sciences waiting room September 2008.

In the Twelfth Five-Year Plan the Indian government committed to establishing universal health coverage and increasing GDP spending on health to 2.5 per cent. Some government schemes have had positive effects on healthcare, such as the National Rural Health Mission Janani Suraksha Yojana (maternal safety scheme) and the Accredited Social Health Activist (ASHA) programme. There are also large NGOs such as the Catholic Health Association of India that cater for underserved populations' health needs. But there remains a pressing need to build upon such initiatives and weave them together into a comprehensive public health service.

In many cases, it is young adults—as people relatively familiar with urban areas where hospitals are located—who navigate the complex field of a commercialized healthcare system on behalf of family members. They leave school or university to assist their families and sometimes have to cut short promising careers. A particular absence of mental healthcare in India also militates against young people's productive engagement with the economy and society. India spends just 0.06 per cent of its health budget

108

on mental health, and yet suicide is now the leading cause of death among 15–29-year-old men in India.

Work

Unemployment and underemployment are major problems in India. Even during the period of fast annual economic growth in India between 2003 and 2009 almost no new jobs were created. In 2015, the number of new jobs actually declined, reaching levels lower than in 2009. This is because a substantial portion of India's economic growth occurred through automation and mechanization, which reduced the labour intensity of manufacturing. Moreover, new service-sector growth did not create large numbers of jobs. For example, the IT sector created 1 million jobs over the 2000s in a country with a working-age population of 700 million. Indeed 1 million young people enter the job market every month. Over 90 per cent of people in India work in the informal economy, where there is little job security, few opportunities for career progression, and an absence of collective bargaining mechanisms.

The official figure for youth unemployment in India—roughly 10 per cent—vastly underestimates the scale of the problem because few young people report themselves as jobless in India. There is no social security available for those out of work and therefore little incentive to register as unemployed. The much more common problem in India is underemployment. People perform work that does not reflect their ambitions and which is often part-time, seasonal, and insecure. In urban areas, young people typically enter service-sector jobs in areas such as marketing, hospitality, retail, and security. In rural areas, young men often enter small-scale work in the areas of transport, sales, education, and work associated with the 'new economy', while young women are more likely to be employed in agriculture.

Underemployment is an identity as well as an economic predicament. Youth in India seek to preserve their status in the face of failing to find their first choice of work. They engage in service-type occupations that continue to signal their educated standing, even if they provide little money, such as volunteering, sometimes without pay, to work in local private schools or starting temporary marketing businesses.

Having spent long periods acquiring educational credentials and seeking other opportunities for advancement in small-scale coaching centres, tutorial institutions, 'personality centres', and other such establishments, young people sometimes respond to the social fact of being shut out of formal, well-paid work by reproducing the system that produced them as underemployed youth. They become involved themselves in running tutorial rackets or bogus private colleges.

A sense of cynicism and disappointment has taken hold in this context. Some young people refer to themselves as engaged only in 'timepass'. They wait for better work while finding ways to stave off boredom and negative introspection. Among low castes and Muslims, the downgrading of expectations that accompanies the period after leaving school or university and the associated frustration of underemployment is often particularly dramatic. In 1970 Ronald Dore labelled India 'the country of the BA bus conductor'. It has now become the country of the MA manual labourer. This is part of a broader malaise, of course, that also affects young people in large parts of sub-Saharan Africa, the Middle East, and China. But it is especially intense in India (Figure 15).

Increases in unemployment and underemployment also impose particular direct and indirect hardships on young women. This directly affects them because young women are often finding that, while their parents had formerly discouraged them from seeking paid employment outside the home, the crisis in men's access to secure salaried work now compels young women to also enter the search for secure paid jobs. The unemployment and

15. Young people at a university in north India in the run-up to student elections, October 2004.

underemployment crisis also affects women via the social institution of arranged marriage. In Hindu families at the point of marriage it is customary in an increasing number of regions of India for a bride's family to pay a groom's family a dowry, often comprising cash and consumer goods, and which often continues after the point of the wedding itself. In some places the dowry is explicitly linked to the bride's family's estimation of the 'value' of the groom, calculated in large part with reference to his current or future occupational status. Families have to pay larger dowries if they wish their daughters to marry into households with a well-paid groom. But this 'system' is plagued with uncertainty. For example, where a groom is promoted or acquires a job after a marriage, his family may ask for an additional dowry payment from the bride's family. In other instances, a bride's family may feel that they were tricked into marrying into a family in which the groom, initially promising, proves to be unemployed. These uncertainties place young women—and to some extent also young men—in vulnerable situations. For example, households may harass a new bride to increase their bargaining power in a quarrel

111

over dowry. More broadly, the problem of employment scarcity seems to encourage a strategic approach to arranged marriages, commodifying the bodies and credentials of young people.

Youth Action

Some young people have become involved in forms of destructive politics in response to the hardships of unemployment and underemployment. Jobless Hindu youth were among the instigators of religious communal violence against Muslims in Bombay in the early 1990s and of political unrest in the north-east of India. They have also been prominent in the communist rebellion that has been developing in central parts of the country. Working largely in tribal and remote areas in eastern India, the current generation of communist Naxalites has fought to expel the state and establish institutions to administer justice and land redistribution. In 2007, at the height of the movement's influence, more than a third of the districts in India were considered 'Maoist affected', and in some regions the Naxalites had almost complete control. The vast majority of Naxalites are under the age of 30.

Another barometer of youth frustration is the continuing tendency of young people to campaign vociferously in opposition to caste reservations. A commentator writing in 1947 or even 1990—at the height of debates around OBC reservations—might have considered rather unlikely the prospect of young people coming out to the streets in the second decade of the 21st century on the issue of positive discrimination. By all accounts, they might have imagined that economic growth and development would progressively reduce the importance of state employment to the country's youth. But the opposite has occurred. Starved of real opportunities in the private sector, youth have refocused on state employment with a new energy. Reservations become a symbolic index of young people's sense of being shut out of possibilities for meaningful advancement.

The disaffection of young people in India has also been evident at the everyday level. Unemployed young men have been prominent in local associations, called 'caste panchayats', that mete out violent and humiliating punishments to those who contravene norms around marriage. Unemployed youth have also been involved in everyday forms of caste discrimination and in the harassment and rape of young women, especially in provincial India.

Yet young people excluded from the benefits of Indian modernity have also responded to disappointment and 'timepass' in more positive ways. As Karl Mannheim pointed out long ago, young people are typically less invested in the status quo relative to older generations—they are less likely to own property, for example. In addition, in India young people are more likely to be educated than older generations, have better access to and understanding of communications technology, and are more familiar with citizenship norms—in this sense, they are embodiments of the 'social revolution'. Moreover, young people, due to their proximity to childhood, often invest their social and political action with a spirit of innovation and even playfulness, unsettling established ideas in the process. In Mannheim's terms, young people have a 'fresh contact' with their surrounding social environment. Human history advances because of the constant emergence of new generations.

The evidence of young people being involved in reactionary activity should caution against romanticizing youth. It is striking that young people in some parts of India are often reinventing strict rules about marrying within caste that older people have forgotten. Youth can be highly conservative, as higher-caste opposition to low-caste reservations also shows.

Yet there is equally a growing body of evidence that suggests that many young people are remaking India in progressive directions, even in the context of disappointment. Youth were instrumental in building up grassroots support for the Aam Aadmi Party. Young people were lead players in many of the political movements that have characterized India's social revolution. For example, they were prominent among Anna Hazare's anti-corruption drive, instilling in that movement a concern for areas of governance that related specifically to young people, such as jobs and education. The involvement of young people in the Right to Education movement also highlights an important point about the potential of youth. Even if young people have not been able to obtain a payoff from schooling in terms of secure employment, they have often been able to draw on their education to critique the system that produced them as unemployed youth.

The everyday ways in which young people have responded to disappointing education, poor job outcomes, and social malaise are equally evident. Young people are heavily involved in NGOs. They are in the vanguard of efforts to use Public Interest Litigation and the Right to Information Act to hold government, unscrupulous corporate agents, and others to account. They also work a great deal under the radar, connecting poor people to the state, motivating others in local society, and acting as role models or helpers in their communities.

In such ways, a power shift is occurring towards the young, who often possess a better understanding of technology and are assuming some of the functions formerly associated with 'village elders', such as resolving conflicts, negotiating with the state, and occupying positions on local panchayat councils. Older people sometimes vigorously contest this power shift, reflecting also intergenerational tensions within families associated with educational failure and unemployment. But elders also often appreciate the role that young people are playing.

Indeed, youth often work as a type of intermediary generation in modern India. Social change is occurring in India so fast that people in their forties and fifties often do not understand the struggles that their children in their pre-teens and teens are experiencing. Youth aged 18–30 fill this gap. They act as tutors for younger children and offer advice and guidance on health, work, and relationships. One comprehensive sociological study undertaken recently by Anirudh Krishna suggests that the availability of a youth role model is the single most important factor governing the educational success of children in rural western India.

Recent anthropologies and sociologies of provincial India also indicate that one of the greatest services that youth leaders provide is their ability to instil hope in others where hopelessness becomes pervasive. They convince people of the need to identify a definite 'future' remote from the present, encourage them to attach value to that future (to formulate goals), and convince them of the possibility or likelihood of achieving those goals (optimism). What these various youth grassroots activities also show is that young people are often those with children's interests closest at heart, reflecting the fact that youth were recently children and often have younger siblings or cousins.

Even if young people have not been able to act as an economic driver of development, they may constitute a 'social dividend'. At the same time, young people themselves counsel against any naive celebration of their work. They would like more secure and well-paid positions in society and greater external support for their social action. They fear the repressive arms of the state.

The story of youth is therefore to some extent the story of India in microcosm. India continues to be characterized by widespread poverty and social inequity, including caste, class, religious, and gender inequalities. This reflects the scale of the problems India faced in 1947 as a result of British imperialism and the inability of post-Independence governments to provide basic social and political guarantees—especially healthcare, education, jobs, policing, and legal help—even in the context of economic growth and reform.

Yet India has thrived as a democracy and is now the world's fastest growing economy. This would have been difficult to predict in 1947, when Britain had impoverished India and when the country seemed divided between a tiny elite and a mass of people disconnected to a large extent from mainstream politics and social commentary. Nehru and his successors have consolidated the idea of India and its territorial integrity. They have built economic and political strength and ensured that this strength contributes to poverty reduction and catalyses socio-cultural expression.

Prempal, Hemlata, Minu, and Afrozi live in the teeth of these contradictions. They often feel downhearted. Reflecting their understanding of the lives of the rich, they see themselves as 'poor' (*garib*), or—in the case of Prempal and Hemlata—'unemployed' or 'underemployed'. Minu and Afrozi argue that village life in the future is likely to become even harder, reflecting a gathering environmental crisis and the strength and depth of social inequalities. For Afrozi, the current central government's neglect of many Muslim social concerns is just one among a number of layers of disappointment and bitterness.

Hope persists, however, because political leaders have addressed some basic needs and the democratic system in India has encouraged aspirations. A social revolution has instilled a sense of being modern, drawn people into civic action, and created a generation of young people who cultivate hope.

Hemlata is representative of this confidence. She has recently acquired a job at a regional newspaper and feels her prospects are 'fairly good'. Her civic activism serves as a beacon for other young women and is generating greater enthusiasm about popular politics in Meerut City.

Prempal is another exemplar. He puts aside his own sense of loss and disappointment to motivate other youth. Prempal believes strongly that you should not rely on politicians or government.

He argues that his own good actions, and those of others like him, can have long-term effects on society. He can utilize the 'demonstration effect', for example by refusing to pay bribes in government offices or speaking politely to bureaucrats.

Despite popular belief, Gandhi never actually said the words—'Be the change you want to see in the world.' But he would surely recognize in such figures as Hemlata and Prempal the notion that individual action can have much broader effects. Certainly, the idea that people can through social effort make a major difference in society is taking root in a wide variety of contemporary Indian contexts. This is partly a matter of people's frustration with government and it has a strong temporal dimension. Citizens want to 'get on with it' and act now to improve their world.

Further reading

Chapter 1: Hope

Dyson, Jane (2014), *Working Childhoods, Youth, Agency and the Environment in India* (Cambridge: Cambridge University Press).

Jeffrey, Craig (2010), *Timepass: Youth, Class and the Politics of Waiting in India* (Stanford, Calif.: Stanford University Press).

Chapter 2: Colonial India: impoverishment

Bates, Crispin (2007), *Subalterns and Raj: South Asia since 1600* (London: Routledge).

Bose, Suguta, and Jalal, Ayesha (2010), *Modern South Asia: History, Culture and Political Economy* (London: Routledge).

Gadgil, Madhav, and Guha, Ramachandra (1993), *This Fissured Land: An Ecological History of India* (Berkeley: University of California Press).

Gandhi, Mohandas Karamchand (1927), *An Autobiography: The Story of my Experiments with Truth* (Ahmedabad: Navajivan).

Guha, Ranajit (1997), *Dominance without Hegemony: History and Power in Colonial India* (Cambridge, Mass.: Harvard University Press).

Keay, John (2010), *India: A History* (London: Harper Collins).

Chapter 3: Colonial India: religious and caste divides

Dirks, Nicholas B. (2002), *Castes of Mind: Colonialism and the Making of Modern India* (Delhi: Permanent Black).

Keay, John (2010), *India: A History* (London: Harper Collins).

Talbot, Ian, and Singh, Gurharpal (2009), *The Partition of India* (Cambridge: Cambridge University Press).

Chapter 4: Making India work? 1947–1989

Corbridge, Stuart, and Harriss, John (2000), *Reinventing India* (Cambridge: Polity Press).

Gopal, Sarvepalli (1984), *Jawaharlal Nehru: A Biography* (London: J. Cape).

Guha, Ramachandra (2007), *India After Gandhi: The History of the World's Largest Democracy* (London: Macmillan).

Kothari, Rajni (2005), *Rethinking Democracy* (Hyderabad: Orient Blackswan).

Chapter 5: Rethinking India

Corbridge, Stuart, Harriss, John, and Jeffrey, Craig (2012), *India Today: Economy, Society and Politics* (Cambridge: Polity).

Fernandes, Leela (2006), *India's New Middle Class* (Minneapolis: University of Minnesota Press).

Jaffrelot, Christophe (2011), *Religion, Caste and Politics in India* (New York: Columbia University Press).

Chapter 6: Social revolution

Chatterjee, Partha (2004), *The Politics of the Governed: Reflections on Popular Politics in Most of the World* (New York: Columbia University Press).

Doron, Assa, and Jeffrey, Robin (2013), *The Great Indian Phone Book: How the Cheap Cell Phone Changes Business, Politics, and Daily Life* (Cambridge, Mass.: Harvard University Press).

Ganti, Tejaswini (2013), *Bollywood: A Guidebook to Popular Hindi Cinema* (London: Routledge).

Manuel, Peter (2014), 'The regional North Indian popular music industry in 2014: from cassette culture to cyberculture', *Popular Music* 33/3, 389–412.

Pankaj, Ashok (2012), *Right to Work and Rural India: Working of the Mahatma Gandhi Rural Employment Guarantee Scheme (MNREGS)* (Delhi: SAGE India).

Roberts, Alasdair (2010), 'A great and revolutionary law? The first four years of India's Right to Information Act', *Public Administration Review* 70/6, 925–33.

Srinivas, Tulasi (2010), *Winged Faith: Rethinking Globalization and Religious Pluralism through the Sathya Sai Movement* (New York: Columbia University Press).

Chapter 7: Youth

Jeffrey, Craig (2010), *Timepass: Youth, Class and the Politics of Waiting in India* (Stanford, Calif.: Stanford University Press).

Jeffrey, Craig, Jeffery, Patricia, and Jeffery, Roger (2008), *Degrees without Freedom? Education, Masculinities, and Unemployment in North India* (Stanford, Calif.: Stanford University Press).

Kapur, Devesh, and Mehta, Pratap Bhanu (eds) (2017), *Navigating the Labyrinth: Perspectives on India's Higher Education* (Delhi: Orient Blackswan).

Mehrotra, Santosh (2015), *Realising the Demographic Dividend: Policies to Achieve Inclusive Growth in India* (Cambridge: Cambridge University Press).

Pinto, Sarah (2008), *Where there is no Midwife: Birth and Loss in Rural India* (New York: Berghahn).

Index

C

D

E

SOCIAL MEDIA
Very Short Introduction

Join our community

www.oup.com/vsi

- Join us online at the official Very Short Introductions
  Facebook page.
- Access the thoughts and musings of our authors with our
  online **blog**.
- Sign up for our monthly **e-newsletter** to receive information
  on all new titles publishing that month.
- Browse the full range of Very Short Introductions online.
- Read **extracts** from the Introductions for free.
- If you are a teacher or lecturer you can order inspection
  copies quickly and simply via our website.